BEHOLD . . . THE MAN!

The Pathway of His Passion

BEHOLD . . . THE MAN!

The Pathway of His Passion

CHARLES R. SWINDOLL

W PUBLISHING GROUP
A Division of Thomas Nelson Publishers
Since 1798
www.wpublishinggroup.com

BEHOLD . . . THE MAN

Published by W Publishing Group, a division of Thomas Nelson, Inc. P.O. Box 141000, Nashville, TN 37214.

Unless otherwise indicated, Scripture quotations used in this book are from the Holy Bible: New Century Version. Copyright © 1987, 1988, 1991 by W Publishing Group, a division of Thomas Nelson, Inc., Nashville, Tennessee 37214. Used by permission.

Other Scripture quotations are from the following sources:

New American Standard Bible (NASB). Copyright © 1960, 1962, 1963, 1968, 1971, 1972, 1973, 1975, 1977 by The Lockman Foundation. Used by permission.

The New Revised Standard Version (NRSV), copyright © 1989 by the Division of Christian Education of the National Council of the Churches of Christ in the USA.

The King James Version of the Bible (KJV).

ISBN 0-8499-4532-1

04 05 06 07 PHX 5 4 3 2 1

Contents

Acknowledgments

Without six people, this book would not have been possible. I want to express my gratitude to each of them.

First, I thank my publishers, Mike Hyatt and David Moberg. From start to finish they stepped up with enthusiasm and a can-do attitude.

Then I thank Brian Goins from our Insight for Living staff for his diligence and creative suggestions as my editor. Well done, good and faithful friend!

Next, I thank Mary Hollingsworth, my managing editor, and her editorial team for their blend of splendid skills and professional seasoned expertise, especially Kathryn Murray, who has designed and typeset so many of my books through the years.

Finally, I thank Carol Spencer, my personal administrator and friend, for her care and persistence in pursuing and obtaining necessary permissions for this book.

If this little volume enables you to *Behold the Man* with a better understanding and greater appreciation, much of the credit goes to them.

PROLOGUE

Behold, the Man!"

Pontius Pilate shouted those words before a bloodthirsty mob at the fortress of Antonia located at Jerusalem in April, AD 33. A Man stood, meek and resigned, before the raucous crowd. Beaten beyond recognition, blood seeping from head to foot, thorns digging in His head, fragments of flesh torn off His body, the carpenter from Nazareth, Jesus, awaited His sentence.

"Crucify Him! Crucify Him!"

He was a long way from Bethlehem's manger. A long way from the tools hanging in Joseph's shop. Days spent sailing the Sea of Galilee with His itinerant band of disciples felt so distant—hearing waves slap against the boat, grilling fish on the shore, swapping stories around the campfire. In His mind, their faces were still fresh from the previous night, reclining around the table for one last meal.

Behold . . . the Man.

Since you are reading this book, chances are you want to encounter the Man who suffered punishment few could imagine, much less endure. Perhaps you heard the story long ago, but the details fogged over with time. Maybe you've recently seen a dramatic portrayal of the events. Down deep you wonder what really happened. What took place on that day some two thousand years ago that still lingers as if it were yesterday?

While reading this book you will find yourself asking the only question that really matters, "Why?" Why would an innocent Man willingly walk toward such a grisly end? Why would He ever accept such mistreatment?

Understanding that answer requires your traveling a painful journey along a road only that Man could take. You and I will get as close as possible, but only He could handle all it included.

The pathway Jesus took in His last twenty-four hours, commonly called "the Passion," started with supper. Then it wove through deep prayers and deals made in darkness. It descended into courts bereft of justice and went through prejudiced rulers stripped of power. On it, Jesus paused for a torturous scourging and plodded to a place called the Skull.

However, as we will discover, it was a pathway He chose rather than one forced on Him.

I believe once you read these few pages, you'll come face to face with Him . . . and you will change. It can happen only as you stop long enough to look . . . to think . . . to imagine.

When you do, when you truly *Behold the Man,* you will never be the same again.

Behold . . . The Man: The Pathway of His Passion

✝

Who would have believed what we heard? Who saw the LORD's power in this? He grew up like a small plant before the LORD, like a root growing in a dry land. He had no special beauty or form to make us notice him; there was nothing in his appearance to make us desire him. He was hated and rejected by people. He had much pain and suffering. People would not even look at him. He was hated, and we didn't even notice him. But he took our suffering on him and felt our pain for us. We saw his suffering and thought God was punishing him. But he was wounded for the wrong we did; he was crushed for the evil we did. The punishment, which made us well, was given to him, and we are healed because of his wounds. We all have wandered away like sheep; each of us has gone his own way. But the LORD has put on him the punishment for all the evil we have done. He was beaten down and punished, but he didn't say a word. He was like a lamb being led to be killed. He was quiet, as a sheep is quiet while its wool is being cut; he never opened his mouth. Men took him away roughly and unfairly. He died without children to continue his family. He was put to death; he was punished for the sins of my people. He was buried with wicked men, and he died with the rich. He had done nothing wrong, and he had never lied. But it was the LORD who decided to crush him and make him suffer. The LORD made his life a penalty offering, but he will still see his descendants and live a long life. He will complete the things the LORD wants him to do. After his soul suffers many things, he will see life and be satisfied. My good servant will make many people right with God; he will carry away their sins. For this reason I will make him a great man among people, and he will share in all things with those who are strong. He willingly gave his life and was treated like a criminal. But he carried away the sins of many people and asked forgiveness for those who sinned.

ISAIAH 53:1–12

1

THE CUP OF SACRIFICE

THE NIGHT BEFORE HE FELT THE NAILS, he gathered twelve friends together around a table . . . and ate.

I've had some pretty amazing meals in my lifetime. They span the extremes, from the sublime to the sensational, from the most primitive to the most formal, fashionable, and elegant. I've been invited to banquets in governors' mansions and have sat at the captain's table on ocean cruises. I've also eaten in rugged missionary huts and around campfires with my family, enjoying delicious fresh-caught fish, and I've tried to choke down hospital meals that tasted like a mixture of wet plaster and soggy cardboard.

Having done more than my share of eating (!) in my more than six decades, I can tell you that, if given a choice, I much prefer a small, intimate setting to a large, impersonal gathering. As a matter of fact, the more I study the New Testament and examine how the people of that era ate their meals, the more I think I would have felt right at home with them, especially among Jesus and His disciples. Almost without exception, they kept their meals simple, and they kept the group small. No five- or six-course feasts. No elegant banquets or flashy decorations. And no formal, sophisticated protocol. Nowhere was this more evident than when they ate the Passover meal together.

Centuries have passed since the evening Jesus sat in the upper room and shared that last simple meal with His disciples. Simple, yet extremely important. During those centuries, that meal has taken on enormous significance. Unfortunately, it has also taken on the trappings of religion—the "extras" of complicated rituals and denominational distinctives. In doing so, it has lost, I believe, some of the profound simplicity that surrounded the table when Jesus and His men met together for supper that final night.

First of all, let's consider why they were together.

> It was almost time for the Feast of Unleavened Bread, called the Passover Feast. The leading priests and teachers of the law were trying to find a way to kill Jesus, because they were afraid of the people. The Day of Unleavened Bread came when the Passover lambs had to be sacrificed. Jesus said to Peter and John, "Go and prepare the Passover meal for us to eat."
>
> —LUKE 22:1–2, 7–8

Every year, on the fourth Thursday of November, many Americans prepare a lavish meal. We invite our nearest and dearest—family and friends—and celebrate the Thanksgiving meal. This is the holiday that remains my all-time favorite of the year. It is a time when we gather for two simple reasons: to have a meal and to remember.

Passover might be considered the Thanksgiving celebration of the Jews. It's not a Thanksgiving with turkey and trimmings, pilgrims and Plymouth Rock, but a time of remembrance of something far more significant.

When the Hebrews were in Egypt, God called Moses to lead them out of slavery and into the Promised Land. On the night of that great Exodus, God told His servant, in effect, "Moses, give these instructions to the Hebrews. Tell each household to choose a perfect lamb—one that is unblemished, without scars or imperfections. They are to take that spotless lamb, kill it in the way I have specified, and drain the blood into a pan. Take that blood and smear it on the doorway of their homes. For tonight, Moses, the Angel of the Lord will visit Egypt. Any home with blood on the door, he will 'pass over' that home and leave it untouched. But if he finds no blood on the door, death will enter that home, and the oldest son will die. There will be no exception, Moses. The Destroyer will 'pass over' only when he sees the blood." (See Exodus 12:1–29.)

That began the single most important of all the Jewish observances. Appropriately, it is called "Passover." God made it clear that they were to remember that epochal night from then on; and when they did, they were to explain its significance to their children. The meal became the Jews' most important celebration.

On His last night with His disciples, Jesus celebrated the Passover, as devout Jews had been doing for centuries. Appropriately, He used that meal of remembrance to turn their attention to His own approaching death.

THE MENU

And they prepared the Passover meal.

—LUKE 22:13

As the Jews celebrated their annual Passover Feast of remembrance and thanksgiving, the required ingredients of that feast were passed down from generation to generation in the traditional teachings of the six hundred thirteen Laws of the Torah. This included the slaughtering and preparing of "the Paschal lamb" (Exodus 12:6); the obligation to eat the Paschal lamb—that is, to participate in the Passover Seder

(Exodus 12:8); the proper preparation of the lamb—it must be roasted (Exodus 12:9); the prohibition against leaving any remains of the Lamb (Exodus 12:10); the requirement to eat matzah (unleavened bread) during Passover (Exodus 12:18); the obligation to tell one's child the story of the liberation from Egypt (Exodus 13:8). These are just a few of the specific instructions from the Torah regarding Passover. Nothing was all that complicated, but what was stated was to be followed to the letter.

The Feast of Passover was centered around three items: roasted lamb, bitter herbs, and unleavened bread. The roasted lamb was central. It was to remind them of the sacrifice of the spotless lamb and the blood spread on the doorposts of believing Hebrew homes. The bitter herbs were a mixture of lettuce, endive, roots, peppermint, and dandelion. As the sting of those bitter herbs touched the tongue, they offered a vivid taste of the stinging years that their Hebrew ancestors had spent in slavery. The unleavened bread was to remind them of the haste with which the Hebrews had to prepare to leave with Moses, their deliverer.

But this night, Jesus created a new tradition: He turned familiar foods into foreboding symbols.

THE MEAL

And when the hour had come, He reclined at the table, and the apostles with Him.

—LUKE 22:14, NASB

At the risk of losing favor with those who are lovers of great works of art, I need to say something that some may not appreciate, and that is this: Leonardo da Vinci did Christianity a great disservice with his painting *The Last Supper*. Not to the world of art, you understand;

artistically his painting is a masterpiece. But historically and biblically the masterpiece is far from authentic.

In da Vinci's painting, Jesus and His disciples are sitting on one side of the table, in chairs, "facing the camera," as it were. But Jesus and the Twelve would not have sat in chairs with high backs at a table some thirty inches from the floor. In the First Century, when people ate a meal, they sat on the floor on small pallets or rugs. In fact, they reclined on their sides, around a table built low to the floor, leaning on one elbow.

Also, they did not eat with utensils, as we do. Bread served as a utensil to sop up or scoop up the other ingredients. Nor was their bread like our common loaf of bread; it was a flat loaf, like our pita bread—and at Passover, made deliberately without the leaven, it was flat and brittle. They would break the bread and dip it into the bitter herbs, then pile on pieces of roasted lamb.

Picture Jesus and His disciples, reclining in a casual circle around a low table, facing each other and eating the Passover meal, as faithful Jews had done for centuries. Those men had eaten that meal, much as Americans have eaten our Thanksgiving meal, all their lives. No surprises. No unexpected moments . . . until Jesus began to speak to them as a group.

> He said to them, "I wanted very much to eat this Passover meal with you before I suffer. I will not eat another Passover meal until it is given its true meaning in the kingdom of God."
>
> —LUKE 22:15–16

The disciples, of course, had no clue how significant this gathering would be. They were barely paying attention, eating the Passover and talking among themselves.

Many folks today view the Twelve as immortal saints of the faith—but at this point in their training, they were very human, sometimes contentious, proud, and competitive. They had no concept of what lay ahead in the coming hours: Jesus would leave them that night and go to the cross, and their faith would later be tested in the fires of persecution.

We'll leave all this for now because I don't want us to drift from where we're headed in this scene as Jesus is with His men around the table.

> While they were eating, Jesus took some bread and thanked God for it and broke it. Then he gave it to his followers and said, "Take this bread and eat it; this is my body." Then Jesus took a cup and thanked God for it and gave it to the followers. He said, "Every one of you drink this. This is my blood which is the new agreement that God makes with his people. This blood is poured out for many to forgive their sins. I tell you this: I will not drink of this fruit of the vine again until that day when I drink it new with you in my Father's kingdom."
> —MATTHEW 26:26–29

They ate together, celebrating the Passover Feast. Traditionally, as devout Jews, they would have been quoting from the ancient Scriptures, remembering the days when their forefathers were enslaved in Egypt and delivered by God through His servant Moses. Suddenly, they noticed that Jesus was no longer participating in the conversation. He looked somber—perhaps more somber than He had looked during all their years together.

As they watched with curiosity, Jesus took a piece of unleavened bread and broke it. Then He bowed His head and prayed. The passage says, "He thanked God for the bread." We don't know specifically what He prayed. Perhaps He asked God that the disciples might begin to sense the significance of that night, the last one He would be spending with them. They didn't know it was the last, but Jesus knew, and He wanted to help them understand what He was about to do . . . and what it would mean to them. Perhaps He prayed for strength in light of what lay ahead. Whatever the untold details might be, we know that having broken the bread and given thanks, He said, "Take this bread and eat it; this is my body."

What? What was He talking about? They must have looked back and forth at each other, confused. Jesus had never said this before. He was suddenly breaking with tradition, leaving them completely shocked.

Theologians, too, have been confused for centuries over that statement. Some have taught that the bread served at the Lord's Table actually becomes the body of Christ when it enters the mouth of the believer. Others believe that when the priest stands before the people and breaks the bread it becomes the body of Christ. Others say that it is *representative*—a spiritual symbol of the body of Christ. I believe that the best answer is the most simple and direct: The bread is a picture of His body, a representation of His body that was given for us on the cross.

In my wallet I carry a small picture of my family. Occasionally, someone will say to me, "We'd love to see your family, Chuck." And I'll reach into my pocket and pull out my family to show them. Not literally, of course; it's just a picture of my family. But I say, "This is my family."

That's what Jesus meant when He said to them that night, "This is my body."

Imagine the stunned silence. Imagine the questions that swarmed through the minds of the disciples: Is He really going to die? Why? What will happen to us? What about the kingdom He promised?

Have all these years with Him been in vain? Their stomachs must have been in knots. The first four books of the New Testament, the gospels, give no indication that a word was spoken in response. For a change, these twelve men sat in stunned silence.

While the taste of the bread was still in their mouths, Jesus picked up a cup of wine. Down through the years people have imagined Jesus using all sorts of cups, from simple clay vessels to elaborate silver chalices. Many myths have surrounded the cup Jesus used at the Last Supper, which some see as a sacred vessel. Those who promote such thinking believe the cup has somehow, somewhere been preserved and venerated through the centuries. Yet God has never wanted His people to worship or venerate any object or person other than Himself. For that reason alone, I'm certain there was nothing elaborate or significant about the cup that Jesus chose on that last night. It was an ordinary, everyday drinking vessel—an earthen vessel, one of several on the table, filled with wine, from which He had been drinking.

Jesus took a cup, offered a prayer of thanks, and said to His disciples, "Every one of you drink this."

I have often asked myself as I read this narrative, for what did Jesus give thanks? He had already asked the blessing on the meal. He had already asked the blessing on the bread. Why pray again? Give thanks for what?

It helps to understand that the same word that is used here for "cup" is used later when Jesus prays in the Garden of Gethsemane: "Father, if it is possible, let this *cup* pass from Me; nevertheless, not as I will, but as You will" (KJV, italics mine). This is also a word that could be used to represent suffering. So as Jesus gave thanks for the cup, He may very well have been giving thanks for the suffering He was facing. And let's not forget that the cup of suffering would include His death on a cruel cross. He knew the path that lay ahead of Him.

> Then Jesus took a cup, gave thanks, and said, "Take this
> cup and share it among yourselves. I will not drink again
> from the fruit of the vine until God's kingdom comes."
>
> —LUKE 22:17–18

These words ended their time together: "You will never celebrate another Passover with Me," Jesus was saying, "but there will come a day when we will celebrate together in My Father's kingdom in the Father's presence."

With cup drained, thoughts lingered around the table. The meal ended with a brief song. Jesus then stood up and without announcement, left the room. They followed.

> Jesus left the city and went to the Mount of Olives, as he
> often did, and his followers went with him.
>
> —LUKE 22:39

Jesus and His disciples made their way out of the city and across the Kidron Valley to a garden along the soft slopes of the Mount of Olives. From what we read in Luke's account, we know Jesus had frequently found quiet refuge in that wooded area . . . quite probably at Gethsemane itself. He did not choose to run and hide, knowing that danger was near, as we would be tempted to do. Instead, He led His men back to that familiar place, unafraid of the capture and arrest that lay ahead. Jesus led His disciples out into a dark night to face the brutal, hostile world that was lurking in the shadows.

✝

A man of sorrows and acquainted with grief.

ISAIAH 53:3, NASB

2

Midnight in the Garden

My aunt ernestine was an accomplished, though self-taught, artist. Of all of her works on canvas, the one I liked best—and the one that intrigued me as a little boy—was a painting of Jesus in the Garden of Gethsemane. It was a large oil painting that hung above the fireplace in my maternal grandparents' home. It was, in fact, the first thing that caught your eye when you walked in the front door.

In the painting, Jesus knelt beside several large boulders, with His hands folded and His arms resting on the rugged rocks, His face looking up into heaven in an attitude of prayer. Above and behind Him rolled a cloudy, troubled sky, moonlit but moody.

One day I pulled over a chair and climbed up, bringing me to the level of the painting. I pressed my nose against the part of the picture that fascinated me—the small droplets of blood coming out of Jesus's forehead. I was bothered by his bleeding. I didn't know the story of Gethsemane then, so I imagined all manner of things. Maybe this Man was lost in the woods and was praying for God to help Him find His way out. But why was His forehead bleeding? Had He hit it on the limbs of the trees as He stumbled through the forest? Or had some enemy struck Him in the face?

One afternoon I asked my granddaddy Lundy, "What does that picture mean?"

He reached down and picked me up, holding me in his arms as we looked together at Aunt Ernestine's painting.

"This is a painting of Jesus when He was in the garden praying before He went to the cross," he said.

"Why is the blood there?" I asked.

"Well, let me show you," said my granddaddy. He got his well-worn Bible and read me the part where it says that Jesus's sweat "was as it were great drops of blood falling down to the ground" during his agonizing prayer in the Garden of Gethsemane (Luke 22:44 KJV).

I never have been able to fully comprehend that kind of agony in prayer, but I believe it happened. Those schooled in medicine call it hematidrosis, where the body can, at times of great stress, so break down that blood can actually ooze through the skin. A careful reading reveals that Luke, a physician as well as author of a gospel, does not write that Jesus actually bled, but that His *sweat* "became as great drops of blood." Whatever it was, no one can overestimate the intense agony that Jesus endured that dark night.

THE HUMANITY OF CHRIST

As we lift the veil and peer into the details, we see just a small portion of a larger picture of the passion of Jesus. ("Passion" is a term commonly used when referring to Christ's suffering between the time of His supper with the disciples and His crucifixion.) What has transpired up to this point? As we saw in the previous chapter, Jesus has been with his followers observing the Passover meal, their last supper together. Judas, the betrayer, has left to accomplish his evil scheme. Now, Jesus and the remaining faithful eleven wind their way through the dimly lit streets of Jerusalem, out through one of the gates of the city, across the southern steps of Herod's temple, down across the Kidron Valley, and on up the Mount of Olives to the dark and thick grove of olive trees called Gethsemane.

Gethsemane is a Hebrew word that means "oil press." Apparently there was a press in the vicinity where olives were crushed for their oil. It was here—alone and in agony—Jesus would endure His most crushing struggle thus far.

> Jesus and his followers went to a place called Gethsemane.
> He said to them, "Sit here while I pray."
> —MARK 14:32

Judging from the ancient olive grove that can be visited today, this must have been a quiet, fragrant, and lovely place. Scholars of the New Testament believe Jesus and His disciples arrived there somewhere between midnight and one o'clock in the morning. Jesus asked His men to sit and wait while He prayed. Apparently they were to be some kind of human shield, guarding the site, lest someone interrupt His time of solitude. He did, however, take three of His closest companions deeper into the garden with Him.

> And He took with Him Peter and James and John, and began to be very distressed and troubled. And He said to them, "My soul is deeply grieved to the point of death; remain here and keep watch." And He went a little beyond them, and fell to the ground, and began to pray that if it were possible, the hour might pass Him by.
> —MARK 14:33–35, NASB

No artist could adequately portray the anguish that began to sweep across Jesus's inner man. Words also fail in trying to describe

His anguish. Here, the Greek words that are translated *very distressed* literally mean "to be struck with terror."

I cannot fully explain the why and how of Jesus's experience. I can only describe what Mark tells us. (Mark was the earliest of the four gospels written, probably written after much time spent with Peter.) Scholars verify that Mark got his information about this night directly from Peter . . . and Peter, of course, was an eyewitness. So from Peter's eyes, through Peter's lips, into Mark's pen come the words "very distressed." An anguishing sense of terror came over Jesus as He faced what lay ahead.

The verse also tells us that He became troubled, "very distressed and troubled." The word *troubled* includes the idea of being "ill at ease, filled with unrest, uncomfortable within." At that moment, just before He fell before the Father in prayer, those feelings closed in on Him. He did not hide His feelings from His three friends—Peter, James, and John. He confessed He was "deeply grieved to the point of death."

What does it mean, in human terms, to be deeply grieved? Think back a moment to a time in your own life that might be described in those words. Maybe it happened when you lost your closest friend. Maybe it came after a long struggle with some addiction that tormented you—the humiliation of being found out and the grief that resulted. Or perhaps it was the untimely death of your mother or father.

I remember the afternoon my father called and said, "Son, I think mother is gone." I immediately drove across the city to my parents' home and there on the sofa was my mother's body. Earlier that afternoon she had decided to take a nap . . . she never awoke. There she lay, lifeless, at the relatively young age of sixty-three. At that moment deep feelings of grief enveloped me.

One writer describes this moment for the Son of God in Gethsemane: "Grief enveloped Him, surrounded Him, saturated His conscious mind. It was so deep it was as if death had wrapped its fingers around His shoulders." Nowhere else in the passion of Jesus can we enter as fully into His humanity as in Gethsemane.

Troubled, distressed, and grieved beyond words, Jesus urged His disciples, "Remain here and stay awake."

Why? Why would He want them to be near Him when He was enduring such anguish? Often the human inclination is to retreat from others when overwhelmed—to hide such feelings. But Jesus didn't hide His anguish from His closest followers. He brought them face to face with all His human emotions. By doing so, He freed them from the temptation to deny their own agonizing feelings in years to come. Even in His torturous struggles, He modeled a life of realistic authenticity.

THE SUBMISSION

Eight of the disciples remained near the entrance to the garden; the other three walked further into the heart of the dark, quiet Garden of Gethsemane with Jesus. Then He said, "Stay right here and wait with Me." And with those words, "He went a little beyond them" and "fell to the ground, and began to pray that if it were possible, the hour might pass Him by."

In the original language in which Mark wrote, both of these verbs indicate continual, constant action. It could actually read like this: "He began falling to the ground and praying, and then falling to the ground and praying, and then falling and praying." In light of that, my Aunt Ernestine and other artists miss what transpired when they portray Jesus kneeling quietly in the moonlight, praying with carefully folded hands. That's not the way it happened. If I read this correctly, Jesus fell on the ground and prayed; He then got up, walked a little further, once again sank to the ground and prayed. He repeated this over and over as, in the anguish of His soul, He continued crying out, *"Abba!"*

> After walking a little farther away from them, Jesus fell to the ground and prayed that, if possible, he would not have this time of suffering. He prayed, "Abba, Father! You can do all things. Take away this cup of suffering. But do what you want, not what I want."
>
> —MARK 14:35–36

In Aramaic, the language Jesus spoke, *abba* was a familiar term for the most intimate relationship between child and parent. The best equivalent in English is the word "daddy." In using that term Mark preserves the sense of intimacy, immediacy, and agony.

"Oh, Daddy!" Jesus is saying. "If it is at all possible, Father, oh, my Father, let this agony that I am facing go by. Let there be another way. All things are possible for You."

Some wonder how Jesus could be fully human and, at the same time, fully divine as God's Son. Simply look and linger at this scene in Gethsemane, where the oil of His anguish was pressed out like the crushed olives. Here, in the darkness of the garden, His humanity gushes out. I'm so grateful that this dark scene has been preserved. Otherwise I fear we would look upon Jesus as some kind of unemotional robot, who went through this divine appointment without any human apprehension or anguish. But it was not like that at all. Jesus was not only undiminished deity, He was also, in every way, true humanity, subject to the identical feelings we have, whether it be joy or sorrow, fear or confidence, exhilarating ecstasy or crushing agony.

At this moment, the totally innocent, sinless Son of God faces and accepts the torture and death that shortly awaits Him. And so He addresses His Father in familiar terms: "If there is any other way to accomplish Your plan, may that come to pass." And then He prays the words that have become the most familiar words in many prayers: "But do what you want, not what I want."

What happened next?

> Then Jesus went back to his followers and found them asleep. He said to Peter, "Simon, are you sleeping? Couldn't you stay awake with me for one hour? Stay awake and pray for strength against temptation. The spirit wants to do what is right, but the body is weak." Again Jesus went away and prayed the same thing. Then he went back to his followers, and again he found them asleep, because their eyes were very heavy. And they did not know what to say to him. After Jesus prayed a third time, he went back to his followers and said to them, "Are you still sleeping and resting? That's enough. The time has come for the Son of Man to be handed over to sinful people. Get up, we must go. Look, here comes the man who has turned against me."
>
> —MARK 14:37–42

Jesus didn't merely offer a brief prayer in the garden and then stand to face His crucifixion. He prayed, and then He went back to the disciples. He then returned to prayer, and then once again came back to the disciples. Three times He went back to pray. This is the struggle of submission: "Not My will, but Yours be done."

What an incredible experience that should have been for the disciples. Yet they missed it. Instead, "He found them sleeping."

The verse says He found "them" sleeping, but He talked to Peter. Do you know why He addressed Peter? Because just a short time before, after the Passover meal, well-meaning Peter had said to Jesus, "Everyone else may stumble in their faith, but I will not" (Mark 14:29). And so He singled out Peter, the very one who had promised, "I will never fall away," and said, "Simon, are you asleep?"

Jesus called him Simon, the disciple's given name, rather than Peter (meaning "rock"), the nickname Jesus had earlier given him. It's almost as if Jesus is implying, "We're back where we started, Simon. You still have a long way to go!" We can't help but wonder how Peter must have felt—the embarrassment of being asked, "Are you sleeping? Couldn't you stay awake for one hour?" Then, graciously, Jesus urges, "Stay awake and pray."

Earlier Jesus had said, "Stay awake." Now He says to Peter, James, and John, "Stay awake and pray." Why? "For strength against temptation." What was that temptation? Surely it was more than just the temptation to fall asleep again. I believe it was the very temptation that they would fall into during the next few hours: the temptation to defect. Right now was the time for the disciples to pray for steel in their souls. Right now was the time for them to stay awake and pray, while there was no enemy around, because when the enemy came, the temptation would be to desert their leader. Jesus told them to stay awake and pray so that might not happen.

An excellent principle of life is implied here: Capitalize on times of peace. Use moments of serenity to cultivate iron-clad convictions, so you won't yield when life gets dicey.

At this moment you may be experiencing tremendous prosperity in your business or peace in your personal life. You may find yourself coasting along, and it looks like a beautiful tomorrow. If so, let me challenge you: Right now you are in the perfect place to prepare yourself. Times of peace and prosperity provide the ideal moments to equip yourself for the inevitable tests of hardship and heartache.

That's what Jesus was saying in Matthew 26:41, "'Stay awake and pray for strength against temptation. The spirit wants to do what is right, but the body is weak.'" This was all too evident, as Jesus returned a third time and found them sleeping.

> And He came the third time, and said to them, "Are you still sleeping and taking your rest? It is enough; the hour has come; behold, the Son of Man is being betrayed into the hands of sinners. Get up, let us be going; behold, the one who betrays Me is at hand!"
> —MARK 14:41–42, NASB

Once again the disciples are sound asleep, maybe even snoring. But now He gently wakes them without rebuke. This is the picture for the artist to portray. Here is unvarnished realism. The disciples have virtually defected already, yet Jesus hovers over them like a mother over a sleeping baby, saying, "It is enough."

He has gone to God in prayer, requesting another alternative, if that were possible. It is not. Now He sees that the only way through is the way of the cross, and He is resigned to it. And with that submissive attitude, He says, "The hour has come . . . the one who betrays Me is at hand."

There's a sense of determined resolve recorded in all four of the gospel accounts. Jesus stands alone in the garden to face His betrayer, Judas, and the hostile multitude. Then, in the flickering torchlight, He is led away as a captive.

This was God's plan. He was willing to accept it.

†

He was hated and rejected by people.

ISAIAH 53:3

3

THREE O' CLOCK
IN THE MORNING

Peter is the disciple with whom we most easily identify, and for good reason. He is so human, so vulnerable, so honest, and at times so downright real that we can see ourselves in his actions and reactions as a disciple. And while I'm on that subject, can you think of anything more embarrassing than for the Bible to include the unadulterated truth of your life for the entire world to read . . . for generations to come? And don't forget: That would also allow centuries of preachers to expose and examine your failures and sins, your outbursts of anger and open denials and embarrassing betrayals, year after year after year. We know Peter well, maybe too well!

To look at this more closely, we must return to the interlude between Jesus's last meal with His disciples in the upper room and His soul-searching struggle in the Garden of Gethsemane. As Jesus and His disciples stumbled through the darkness from Jerusalem to the Mount of Olives, He made some striking and startling comments.

STRONG WORDS BETWEEN TWO FRIENDS

And Jesus said to them, "You will all become deserters; for it is written,

'I will strike the shepherd,
and the sheep will be scattered.'
But after I am raised up, I will go before you to
Galilee."

Peter said to him, "Even though all become deserters,
I will not."

Jesus said to him, "Truly I tell you, this day, this very
night, before the cock crows twice, you will deny me three
times."

But he said vehemently, "Even though I must die with
you, I will not deny you." And all of them said the same.

—MARK 14:27–31, NASB

"After I am raised up," Jesus said. But it is apparent Peter didn't
pay attention to this prediction of His resurrection. All Peter heard
was that they would "all become deserters." The word *deserters*—or as
the New American Standard Bible (NASB) translates it, "You will all
fall away"—is taken from the Greek term meaning "to stumble."

"Every one of you is going to turn against Me, depart from Me,
leave Me . . . all of you will stumble."

And you can almost hear Peter say, with a sweeping gesture of his
rugged fisherman hands toward the other disciples, in his familiar
over-confident tone of voice, "All these others in the group may
desert you, but I certainly will not!"

"Ah, Peter, but you will," responds Jesus with a sigh. He then adds
a comment that must have stung: "Truly I tell you . . . this very night,
before the cock crows twice, you will deny me three times."

Jesus makes three penetrating statements: Peter will deny Him;
Peter will deny Him that very night; and Peter will, in fact, deny Him
three times.

I've often said that Peter suffered from foot-in-mouth disease.

(Sound familiar?) He was given to boasting and overstatement because of an elevated opinion of himself. But let's give him the benefit of the doubt here. Perhaps he was genuinely self-assured. He really meant it! Confident of his own loyalty, his own devotion to Jesus, he didn't mind stepping up and sounding as loyal as he felt. He fully believed he was devoted enough to die with Him, and he said so.

After their Passover meal together and some of the things Jesus had said to them, all the disciples' emotions were high. Obviously Peter's ran even higher. "Lord, the world can come to an end before I'll deny You. All of these others may, but not I!"

And Jesus said, "No, this very night you're going to deny Me. Not once, but three separate times, before the cock crows twice."

William Barclay offers unexpected insight regarding Jesus's mention of the cock crowing.

> It may well be that the cock-crow was not the voice of a bird; and that from the beginning it was not meant to mean that. After all, the house of the High Priest was right in the centre of Jerusalem. And there was not likely to be poultry in the centre of the city. There was, in fact, a regulation in the Jewish law that it was illegal to keep cocks and hens in the Holy City because they defiled holy things. But the hour of 3 a.m. was called *cock-crow,* and for this reason. At that hour the Roman guard was changed in the Castle of Antonia; and the sign of the changing of the guard was a *trumpet call.* The Latin for that trumpet call was *gallicinium,* which means *cock-crow.* It is at least possible that just as Peter made his third denial the trumpet from the castle battlements rang out over the sleeping city . . . and Peter remembered; and thereupon he went and wept his heart out.[1]

The Romans divided each day into three-hour segments called "hours." The three-hour segments of the night were called "watches." These watches determined the three-hour periods of guard duty, just as we have hours of guard duty in military service today. The night watches could also be used to indicate at which hour something occurred. The first night watch began at 6:00 p.m. and went until 9:00; the second watch was from 9:00 p.m. until midnight; the third watch was from midnight until 3:00 a.m.; and the fourth watch was from 3:00 until 6:00 a.m.

The Jews frequently used an abbreviated form when referring to these watches of the night. We find an example of this in Mark 13:35–37, NRSV:

> Therefore, keep awake—for you do not know when the master of the house will come, in the evening, or at midnight, or at cock-crow, or at dawn, or else he may find you asleep when he comes suddenly. And what I say to you I say to all: Keep awake."

"Evening" referred to the end of the first watch, or nine o'clock. "Midnight" was the end of the second watch. Did you notice? "Cock-crow" was their term for the end of the third watch, or 3:00 in the morning. And "dawn" marked the end of the fourth watch.

When Jesus said, "before the cock crows twice," He was referring to the end of the third watch. If Barclay's suggestion is correct, a signal was given in the very early hours of the morning, marking the end of the third watch, and this signal was called "cock-crowing." Except, as we've seen, in this case it wasn't a rooster, but a trumpeter. At the changing of the guard for the next watch, there was a shrill sound of the trumpet. And during festival times, because of the vast numbers of people in the city, frequently two blasts were sounded, one in one direction and one in the other.

Since this was Passover, the trumpeter would have sounded twice. So that's what Jesus meant when He said to Peter, "This very night, before you hear those two blasts on the trumpet, you will have denied Me three times." This also assures us that Peter's third and final denial took place before 3:00 in the morning.

> But Peter insisted, "I will never say that I don't know you! I will even die with you!" and all the other followers said the same thing.
>
> —MARK 14:31

The others soon picked up the refrain of this loyal, yet vulnerable disciple. "Me too." "That's right, Peter, me too." "I will not deny You, Jesus." They were all so loyal, there in the safety of the quiet, sheltered garden . . . in the comfort of their inner circle. Little did they realize what faced them beyond that garden, at 3:00 in the eerie morning darkness of the soul.

For the moment, however, they had only to stay awake and wait as Jesus passed through His own time of agony, His own Gethsemane. All He asked them to do was to "sit here while I pray" and "keep awake." However . . .

> Then Jesus went back to his followers and found them asleep. He said to Peter, "Simon, are you sleeping? Couldn't you stay awake with me for one hour?
>
> —MARK 14:37

He came and found Peter, James, and John sleeping. But it is worth noting that He only addressed one of "them." He singled out Peter. Why? Because Peter was the one who earlier that same evening had declared so boldly, "Even though all the rest fail You, I will not!"

And yet here he was, snoring away. He was too weak either to keep watch or to stay awake. But let's not be too hard on Peter. Who among us hasn't made the same error? We come on strong in the morning and overcommit, only to flame out before nightfall.

Furthermore, Peter wasn't alone when it came to defection. Only a short time later, when Judas arrived to betray Jesus into the hands of His enemies, we witness the sad reality: "Then all of Jesus's followers left him and ran away" (Mark 14:50).

Everyone who had earlier said, "I will never leave You, Jesus. I will never betray You . . . I will never deny You. . . . I will never fail You . . . though everyone else may turn away, I will not," blew it! Every last one of the remaining eleven ran away—deep into the night of obscurity and anonymity. "Then all of Jesus's followers left him and ran away." They scattered like frightened mice.

Peter's Darkest Hour

The people who arrested Jesus led him to the house of the high priest, where all the leading priests, the older Jewish leaders, and the teachers of the law were gathered. Peter followed far behind and entered the courtyard of the high priest's house. There he sat with the guards, warming himself by the fire.

—Mark 14:53–54

Peter had fled with the others when Jesus was arrested in Gethsemane. Yet he did not go far. He followed Jesus and His captors from "far behind." Standing back in the shadows in the cold morning hours, Peter watched everything unfold. He followed the crowd right into the courtyard of the high priest. The soldiers were gathered around a small fire, and carefully, with his cloak wrapped closely around his face, Peter approached the embers to warm himself.

Afraid but curious, Peter's loyalty was at war with his fear. And so he followed Jesus at a safe distance.

> The leading priests and the whole Jewish council tried to find something that Jesus had done wrong so they could kill him. But the council could find no proof of anything. Some of the people there began to spit at Jesus. They blindfolded him and beat him with their fists and said, "Prove you are a prophet!" Then the guards led Jesus away and beat him.
>
> —MARK 14:55, 65

Jesus was tormented, humiliated, spit upon, cursed, and falsely accused. He stood there silent and bleeding. Then they began to mock Him. They blindfolded Him and slapped His face, challenging Him to "Prove you are a prophet! Tell us who hit you!" And off in the shadows, taking it all in, stood frightened Peter, haunted by the memory of his own words: "I will never deny You, Jesus. Though all others fall away, I won't fail You." They pulsated in his mind. He frowned, unable to silence the condemnation of his own conscience.

> While Peter was in the courtyard, a servant girl of the high priest came there. She saw Peter warming himself at the fire and looked closely at him. Then she said, "You also were with Jesus, that man from Nazareth."
>
> —MARK 14:66–67

Perhaps someone poked the fire, causing it to blaze up and flash light across Peter's face. At that moment a servant girl from the household of the high priest recognized him. Possibly she had seen Peter, sometime earlier, walking alongside Jesus and the disciples through the streets of Jerusalem, where the group had become a familiar sight.

"You are one of the Nazarene's followers," the girl said. Whether it was said accusingly or assuredly, we are not told. Regardless of her tone, however, Peter conveniently forgot his earlier promise.

> But Peter said that he was never with Jesus. He said, "I don't know or understand what you are talking about." Then Peter left and went toward the entrance of the courtyard. And the rooster crowed.
>
> —Mark 14:68

This was a bold, flat-out denial—nothing subtle about it. Peter then removed himself to an even safer distance. And with that, he withdrew further as he took another step down to calm all suspicion . . . and he took yet another, for the serving maid wouldn't give up.

> The servant girl saw Peter there, and again she said to the people who were standing nearby, "This man is one of those who followed Jesus." Again Peter said that it was not true.
>
> —Mark 14:69–70

This time the young woman addressed the crowd standing nearby. "Listen, this is one of them." And once again Peter openly denied any association with Jesus of Nazareth.

> Again Peter said that it was not true.
>
> —Mark 14:70

How did they know Peter was from Galilee? As Matthew's gospel says, "The way you talk shows it" (26:73). Most Galileans found it difficult to pronounce some of the gutturals in the dialect spoken in Jerusalem at the time. Native Judeans picked up on that. Also, Galileans were sometimes considered ignorant and unlearned people. The Romans, especially public officials, usually spoke several languages, but the Galileans were, at best, bilingual. Thus, when Peter barked out, "I'm not! I do not know Him! I do not understand what you're talking about," the bystanders easily spotted him as Galilean.

Our speech often betrays us. A number of years ago my wife and I were enjoying a lovely evening at one of the finest restaurants in the city of Dallas. In keeping with the décor, the servers wore the attire of North Africa. We felt as if we were in old Morocco until the young woman assigned to our table walked over and asked, "Y'all ordered y'all's dranks yet?"

At that moment we knew we were still in Texas.

If you encounter a New Englander anywhere in the world, they will want to "pahk the cah in the yahd." And people from the state of "New Joisey" usually give themselves away. We mark ourselves by our speech. So it's not difficult to understand why the bystanders identified Peter as a Galilean.

At that point, Peter reverted to the lowest form of speech in any language: profanity.

> But he began to curse and swear, "I do not know this man you are talking about!" And immediately a cock crowed a second time. And Peter remembered how Jesus had made the remark to him, "Before a cock crows twice, you will deny Me three times." And he began to weep.
>
> —MARK 14:71–72, NASB

This could mean that he blasphemously called down curses from God: "If I am a liar, may God strike me dead." Or perhaps he used the vulgar talk of the fishing trade, his former life, as if to say, "Don't connect me with the Nazarene's disciples."

Whatever form this cursing and swearing took, it was effective. His finger-pointing critics backed off.

But his curses had scarcely fallen from his lips before two things occurred that shook Peter to the core. First, the trumpet sounded the end of the third watch. And then it sounded again. The shrill blast of cock-crow . . . twice! Surely that sent a chill up Peter's spine.

For the second, we must turn to Luke's gospel:

> But Peter said, "Man, I do not know what you are talking about!" At that moment, while he was still speaking, the cock crowed.
>
> And the Lord turned and looked at Peter. Then Peter remembered the word of the Lord, how he had said to him, "Before the cock crows today, you will deny me three times."
>
> —LUKE 22:60–61, NRSV

We're not told where Jesus was standing, but wherever He was, He had a clear view of Peter out on the porch. For at the loud blast of the *gallicinium,* which pierced the night air, "the Lord turned and looked at Peter." At that instant Peter remembered what Jesus had predicted: "Truly I tell you, this day, this very night, before the cock crows twice, you will deny me three times." Talk about humiliation!

What was the look? Was it a look of surprise? No. Jesus had told Peter that he was going to betray Him. Was it a look of anger and rejection? Never. I think it must have been a look of sorrow and enormous disappointment: "What have you done, Peter? You've numbered yourself among these, my enemies and betrayers. You've done exactly as I said you would, Peter. Oh, my longtime friend, think of what you have done."

It was not a look of rage or indifference or even surprise, but a look of mixed emotions: aching sorrow and wounded love—a love that had not ended, despite Peter's open and repeated denials, a love that would not let him go. Peter saw loving, unmerited grace in Jesus's eyes, and it melted him to tears.

Then Peter lost control of himself and began to cry.
—MARK 14:72

Not one of us can look with judgment upon Peter. Why? Because in the violent mayhem of that evening, we too would have denied Jesus.

Not only was He deserted by his closest friends, but that same night justice itself fled from Jesus in six different trials.

†

Men took him away roughly and unfairly.

ISAIAH 53:8

4

THE SIX TRIALS OF JESUS

MANY PEOPLE have never made a serious study of what transpired immediately before Jesus's crucifixion. They tend to jump
from Gethsemane to Golgotha, omitting most, if not all, the events
in between. In making that leap, they lose much of the history and
theology, not to mention the local color of Jesus's era; as a result, they
overlook important details that led to the final verdict against Jesus.

Put bluntly, the trials that resulted in Jesus of Nazareth's being
nailed to a cross provide the classic example of an unfair and illegal
rush to judgment. Biased and fallacious in every way, these trials represent the darkest day in the history of jurisprudence. The accused was
the only perfect and completely innocent person who has ever lived.
Yet He was declared guilty ... guilty of crimes He never committed.
Tragically, His alleged crimes resulted in His being condemned to the
most painful form of capital punishment ever devised. Death for a
capital offense, according to first-century Roman law, was crucifixion.

Later we will discover why the trials, suffering, death, and subsequent
resurrection of Christ are, in fact, the bedrock truth of Christianity,
forming the foundation of the faith. Because this is true, I am all
the more surprised at how few followers of Jesus have carefully,

thoughtfully, and thoroughly studied the events surrounding His death, particularly the trials He endured. Yes, trials . . . not one, but six.

AN ISSUE OF TIME

Before we take a careful look at these events, we need to review the chronology, both in terms of time and in terms of the unfolding of events as recorded in the gospels.

In the Roman world—the Gentile world—time was reckoned from midnight to midnight (as we measure time today). One second after midnight began the new day, and the day ended at the stroke of midnight. From midnight to midnight was one day. According to the Jewish calendar, however, the new day began at one second past six o'clock in the evening, and the day ended at the stroke of six o'clock the next evening. From six o'clock in the evening to six o'clock the next evening was one day.

In the previous chapter, we learned that the nighttime hours were measured by "watches." Between six in the evening and six in the morning, the time was divided into four watches of three hours each. You'll recall, the first watch was from six to nine, the second from nine to midnight, the third from midnight to three, and the fourth from three to six in the morning.

From six in the morning until six in the evening, the day was divided into "hours." For example, in Matthew's record of the crucifixion, he refers to two different times of the day: "Now from the sixth hour darkness fell upon all the land until the ninth hour" (Matthew 27:45, NASB).

If you reckon time with the Jewish day beginning at 6:00 a.m., then the sixth hour would be noon. Therefore, Matthew writes that at noon darkness fell across the sky and cast an ominous shadow over the earth until the ninth hour, or three in the afternoon. That represented three full hours of darkness in the middle of the day.

THE IMPORTANT EVENTS

Now, with an understanding of this dual measurement of time (Jewish and Gentile), let's take a look at the events surrounding the death of Christ. You can also follow along using the chart on page 43.

Jesus and His disciples left the upper room in the evening, following their Last Supper together, and went to the Garden of Gethsemane, where Jesus prayed and His disciples slept. We can't say exactly what time it was, but it was probably after midnight when Jesus began praying, sometime during the third watch of the night (midnight to three). How long Jesus prayed we don't know, but long enough for him to return three different times and find the disciples sleeping.

Judas and the mob must have arrived on the scene sometime after 1:00 a.m. Then began the series of six trials:

1. The first trial took place at the residence of Annas, the former high priest. That took place about 2:00 a.m.

2. A second unofficial trial was held at the home of his son-in-law, Caiaphas, around 3:00 a.m.

3. Next came the third trial, a formal hearing before the Sanhedrin—the seventy men who formed the Supreme Court of the Jews. The gospel narrative states that this took place "when it was day." Thus, we can assume that this third trial must have been around 6:00 a.m.

4. It was at His fourth trial, about 6:30 or 7:00 a.m., "when morning had come," that Jesus had His first interrogation by Pilate, the leading Roman official.

5. Shortly after that there was an audience before Herod Antipas, the tetrarch or governor of Galilee. That was His fifth trial.

6. Herod then sent Jesus back to Pilate for a second and final time . . . trial number six.

By 8:00 in the morning Jesus had undergone all six trials. A rush to judgment? You decide.

By 9:00 a.m., "the third hour," Jesus had traveled the *Via Dolorosa* (or Way of Sorrow), from the place of scourging to Golgotha, the public place of the skull. There He was nailed to the cross. At noon, darkness fell over the earth as He hung there, dying. Finally, at 3:00 in the afternoon, or "about the ninth hour," Jesus breathed His last and "finished" His mission.

OVERALL ILLEGAL MANEUVERINGS

Let's review those illegal maneuverings in greater detail.

Jesus's first three trials were *religious* in nature. The accusation was blasphemy, which was an offense that was admissible only in a Jewish court of law. So when Jesus stood before Annas, Caiaphas, and the Sanhedrin (trials one, two, and three), He was accused of blasphemy.

But the charge of blasphemy meant nothing in a Roman court of law. Romans had many gods. To a people with so many gods, blasphemy was meaningless. Therefore, when Jesus was brought before Pilate and Herod for the three *civil* trials, the charge had to be changed (an illegal act in itself). Then Jesus was accused of treason and labeled an insurrectionist by His accusers. If it could be proven that He was guilty of trying to overthrow the government of Caesar, then He would be put to death.

As I stated at the beginning of this chapter, there has never been a greater sham than the trials of Jesus Christ. Three religious trials and three civil trials . . . and all six were illegal. Let me explain.

A trial was never to be held at night, yet the first two were. The accused was allowed to have an attorney speak on his or her behalf, yet Jesus was never allowed a defense attorney. The accused could not

CHRONOLOGY OF EVENTS	
Event	**Approximate Time**
Prayer and agony at Gethsemane (Matthew, Mark, Luke)	1:00 a.m.
Betrayal by Judas and arrest of Jesus (Mark 14:43–46; John 18:12)	1:30 a.m.
Irregular, unauthorized inquiry at Annas's residence (John 18:13–23)	2:00 a.m.
Unofficial trial at Caiaphas's residence (Matthew 26:57–68; John 18:24)	3:00 a.m.
Formal, official trial before Sanhedrin in their chamber to confirm capital sentence (Mark 15:1; Luke 22:66–71)	6:00 a.m. ("when it was day")
First interrogation by Pilate at official residence (Matthew 27:1–2, 11–14; Luke 23:1–7; John 18:28–38)	6:30 a.m. ("when morning had come . . . and it was early")
Audience/mockery before Herod (Luke 23:8–12)	7:00 a.m.
Final judgment of Pilate (All Gospels)	7:30 a.m.
Scourging in Praetorium (All Gospels)	8:00 a.m.
Nailing of hands and feet to the cross (All Gospels)	9:00 a.m. ("it was the third hour")
Darkness (Matthew, Mark, Luke)	12:00 Noon ("when the sixth hour had come, darkness fell")
Death of Jesus (All Gospels)	3:00 p.m. ("and at the ninth hour")

In less than twenty-four hours, Jesus goes from arrest to execution.

be declared guilty without *reputable* witnesses, yet those who accused Christ were *false* witnesses.

In the greatest travesty of justice, Jesus was *declared* guilty but never *proven* guilty. As you may recall, Pilate, the same man who finally said, "Take Him and do with Him as you wish," had earlier said, "I find no fault in Him at all." Of all the people before whom Jesus stood, the only one who gave Him even the slightest measure of justice was Pilate, who said up to the end, "I find no fault in this man."

The Jews followed the Mosaic Law, interpreted for them in the Talmud, the legal handbook of that day, while the Romans were guided by the Roman code of criminal procedure. These documents set the boundaries, and they allowed for no "gray" areas. For example, the Jewish court could not hear testimony regarding a capital crime during the hours of darkness. The language of the code read: "The members of the court may not alertly and intelligently hear the testimony against the accused during darkness."

Did the men who tried Jesus know that? Of course they did. These men formed the Sanhedrin; they were teachers of the Law. Yet they deliberately broke the Law.

Another legal detail relates to the factor of time. Members of the Jewish court, after hearing the testimony in a capital crime, were not permitted to render an immediate verdict. They were required to adjourn to their homes for two days and two nights. They were to eat light food, drink light wines, and sleep well, and once again return and hear the testimony against the accused. Then, and only then, could they vote.

One more small detail—but another illegal act. The code required that the Sanhedrin must vote one person at a time, and that the youngest members must vote first, so they would not be influenced by the older members. In Jesus's trial before the Sanhedrin, given the speed by which it all transpired, we are safe to assume that all voted quickly, emotionally, and simultaneously.

In the chart "The Trials of Jesus Christ" on page 46, I have noted the officiating authority, the Scripture references, the accusations, the legality, the type, and the result of each of the six trials. This should help you pursue your own in-depth study of these events.

To understand why there were two phases, religious and civil, of three trials each, we need to look a little further at Jewish and Roman law. The Jews were allowed to bring the Jewish people before their own religious leaders/judges/court system, but the Jews were not allowed, under Roman law, to take a person's life. That required permission from Rome, which explains why the proud members of the Sanhedrin would appeal to Pilate—to Rome. They hoped he would find Jesus guilty and pronounce the death sentence. That's why Jesus was not stoned to death. If He had been put to death under Jewish Law, He would have been stoned. But under Roman law in the first century, as mentioned earlier, capital punishment meant death by crucifixion.

THE FIRST TRIAL: JESUS BEFORE ANNAS

It's time to meet the main players in this drama of injustice. In doing this, we will look at the trials of Jesus as described by the four gospel writers. Since the different writers offer unique observations and insights on what occurred, it is helpful—in fact, essential—that we take all of them into consideration as we reconstruct these events.

> Then the soldiers with their commander and the Jewish guards arrested Jesus. They tied him and led him first to Annas, the father-in-law of Caiaphas, the high priest that

THE TRIALS OF JESUS CHRIST

Trial	Officiating Authority	Scripture	Accusation	Legality	Type	Result
1	Annas, ex-high priest of the Jews (AD 6–15)	John 18:13–23	Trumped-up charges of irreverence to Annas.	ILLEGAL! Held at night. No specific charges. Prejudice. Violence.	Jewish and Religious	Found guilty of irreverence and rushed to Caiaphas.
2	Caiaphas—Annas's son in-law—and the Sanhedrin (AD 18–36)	Matthew 26:57–68 Mark 14:53–65 John 18:24	Claiming to be the Messiah, the Son of God—blasphemy (worthy of death under Jewish law).	ILLEGAL! Held at night. False witnesses. Prejudice. Violence.	Jewish and Religious	Declared guilty of blasphemy and rushed to the Sanhedrin (supreme court).
3	The Sanhedrin—seventy ruling men of Israel (their word was needed before He could be taken to Roman officials).	Mark 15:1a Luke 22:66–71	Claiming to be the Son God—blasphemy.	ILLEGAL! Accusation switched. No witnesses. Improper voting.	Jewish and Religious	Declared guilty of blasphemy and rushed to Roman official, Pilate.
4	Pilate, governor of Judea, who was already in "hot water" with Rome (AD 26–36).	Matthew 27:11–14 Mark 15:1b–5 Luke 23:1–7 John 18:28–38	Treason (accusation was changed, since treason worthy of capital punishment in Rome).	ILLEGAL! Christ was kept under arrest, although He was found innocent. No defense attorney. Violence.	Roman and Civil	Found innocent . . . but rushed to Herod Antipas; mob over-ruled Pilate.
5	Herod Antipas, governor of Galilee (4 BC–AD 39).	Luke 23:8–12	No accusation was made.	ILLEGAL! No grounds. Mockery in courtroom. No defense attorney. Violence.	Roman and Civil	Mistreated and mocked; returned to Pilate without decision made by Herod.
6	Pilate (second time).	Matthew 27:15–26 Mark 15:6–15 Luke 23:18–25 John 18:29–19:6	Treason, though not proven (Pilate bargained with the mob, putting Christ on a level with Barabbas, a criminal)	ILLEGAL! Without proof of guilt, Pilate allowed an innocent man to be condemned.	Roman and Civil	Found innocent, but Pilate "washed his hands" and allowed Him to be crucified.

year. Caiaphas was the one who told the Jews that it would be better if one man died for all the people.

—JOHN 18:12–14

The first of Jesus's six trials took place at the residence of Annas, the former high priest (perhaps he was considered as sort of a high priest emeritus). Annas was also the father-in-law of Caiaphas, the present high priest.

Annas had served as high priest from AD 6 to AD 15. So why would the mob take Jesus to this man who had been out of office for more than fifteen years?

Apparently the Jews—at least the ones in this "mob justice" crowd—viewed Annas as the final authority. If we are correct in viewing Annas as high priest emeritus, then it would stand to reason that the Jews would respect him as an elder statesman; therefore, protocol demanded that he be consulted first. No doubt politics played a role in all this. Keep in mind that his son-in-law, Caiaphas, was now high priest.

I don't think they had to drag Annas out of bed; I doubt that he was surprised by their visit. Certainly nothing is said of his having to be awakened. I believe he was waiting for them . . . that all of this had been arranged beforehand, set up as part of the plot to condemn Jesus.

This kangaroo court, held illegally in the very early hours of the morning and in a private residence, was not a spur-of-the-moment event. It was all carefully orchestrated.

> The high priest asked Jesus questions about his followers and his teaching. Jesus answered, "I have spoken openly to everyone. I have always taught in synagogues and in the Temple, where all the Jews come together. I never said anything in secret. So why do you question me? Ask the

people who heard my teaching. They know what I said."

When Jesus said this, one of the guards standing there hit him. The guard said, "Is that the way you answer the high priest?"

Jesus answered him, "If I said something wrong, then show what it was. But if what I said is true, why do you hit me?"

—JOHN 18:19–23

This blow is only the beginning of a night of violence and senseless brutality. Along with the other illegalities, violence is now permitted in the courtroom. Jesus asks for truth and justice and is given physical abuse and lies. "If I am not telling the truth," He says, "provide a witness. But if I am telling the truth, why do you strike me?" The first trial ends with an unanswered, albeit excellent and relevant question.

This is the first of many questions never answered. The irony, of course, is that it is not really Jesus who is on trial; it is all those around Him.

The Second Trial: Jesus Before Caiaphas

Annas ignored Jesus's question and "Then Annas sent Jesus, who was still tied, to Caiaphas the high priest." Trial number two is about to begin.

Those people who arrested Jesus led him to the house of Caiaphas, the high priest, where the teachers of the law and the older Jewish leaders were gathered.

The leading priests and the whole Jewish council tried to find something false against Jesus so they could kill him. Many people came and told lies about him, but the council could find no real reason to kill him. Then two people came and said, "This man said, 'I can destroy the Temple of God and build it again in three days.'"

Then the high priest stood up and said to Jesus, "Aren't you going to answer? Don't you have something to say about their charges against you?" But Jesus said nothing.

Again the high priest said to Jesus, "I command you by the power of the living God: Tell us if you are the Christ, the Son of God."

Jesus answered, "Those are your words. But I tell you, in the future you will see the Son of Man sitting at the right hand of God, the Powerful One, and coming on clouds in the sky."

When the high priest heard this, he tore his clothes and said, "This man has said things that are against God! We don't need any more witnesses; you all heard him say these things against God. What do you think?"

The people answered, "He should die."

Then the people there spat in Jesus' face and beat him with their fists. Others slapped him. They said, "Prove to us that you are a prophet, you Christ! Tell us who hit you!"

—MATTHEW 26:57,59–68

Isn't it interesting that everyone seems to be awake and alert this late at night? It is now about 3:00 in the morning, yet they are all wide awake, assembled, and waiting. It is nothing other than a pre-arranged scenario—a plot.

Caiaphas was a puppet of Rome. Although he was the moderator and ruling member of the Sanhedrin, and his word was taken as law among the Jews, he and his cohorts were seeking people to bear false witness against Jesus. These officials, supposedly fair-minded men of reputation, called to uphold justice within the courts of the Temple, were prejudiced judges, looking for people who would lie.

The problem was, they were shy of witnesses against Jesus. Angered by the situation and by Jesus's brief but quiet responses, Caiaphas cut the trial short, judging Him deserving of death, and allowing the accused to be physically humiliated and abused.

The Third Trial: Jesus before the Council of Elders

Caiaphas then sent Jesus to the Sanhedrin—also called "the Council of Elders"—the seventy men who sat in ultimate authority over the Jews. This represents the third trial.

> When it was day, the Council of elders of the people assembled, both chief priests and scribes, and they led Him away to their council chamber, saying, "If You are the Christ, tell us." But He said to them, "If I tell you, you will not believe; and if I ask a question, you will not answer. But from now on THE SON OF MAN WILL BE SEATED AT THE RIGHT HAND of the power OF GOD."
>
> And they all said, "Are You the Son of God, then?" And He said to them, "Yes, I am."
>
> And they said, "What further need do we have of testimony? For we have heard it ourselves from His own mouth."
>
> —LUKE 22:66–71, NASB

Some critics of the Scriptures have said that Jesus never claimed He was the Son of God. Yet I would like to know what Luke 22:70 means if it doesn't mean that? Perhaps He did not say the words directly: "I am the Son of God." But when Caiaphas asked Him, "Are You the Son of God?" He answered, without hesitation, "Yes, I am." In declaring His identity He verifies His deity.

That declaration was all the Sanhedrin needed. Without even attempting to examine any evidence or probe into His spotless record, they accused Jesus of blasphemy and prepared to take Him before Pilate, the Roman governor. But remember this: Blasphemy was a *religious* charge; it meant nothing in a Roman courtroom, which is why the Jewish leaders changed the charges against Jesus. The accusation of blasphemy would not be mentioned again, because it would carry no weight in swaying Pilate's opinion. The charge would now be switched to insurrection and treason. Jesus, they would say, was trying to overthrow the government of Rome. An interesting accusation in light of the fact that it was Jesus who publicly taught people to "'render to Caesar the things that are Caesar's; and to God the things that are God's'"(Matthew 22:21). They conveniently forgot that, however, when they went before the civil court in Jesus's fourth trial.

THE FOURTH TRIAL: JESUS BEFORE PILATE

> Very early in the morning, the leading priests, the older leaders, the teachers of the law, and all the Jewish council decided what to do with Jesus. They tied him, led him away, and turned him over to Pilate, the governor.
> —MARK 15:1

This brings us to the next player in our drama and probably the most fascinating character of all: Pontius Pilate.

Pilate was the Roman governor, or procurator, over Judea. He was not a Caesar. Tiberius was the Caesar, the Imperial Emperor of the

Roman Empire, ruling from his headquarters in Rome. Pilate was one of his many regional representatives, the governor of Judea.

Normally Pilate resided at his comfortable and beautiful palace on the Mediterranean coast in Caesarea, but he was in Jerusalem during Passover because the crowds were so large. His presence, His entourage, and the soldiers who came with him were there to help maintain law and order in the streets of Jerusalem.

Now there is something we need to understand about Pilate, because there is quite a discrepancy between the way Pilate is depicted in the history books and the way he is portrayed by the writers of the gospels. In the Scriptures, Pilate vacillates. He is shifting, uneasy, seemingly eager to please the people—in particular, the Jews. The Pilate in the pages of history books looks nothing like that.

Pilate was an anti-Semitic Gentile, Roman to the core. He was an absolute wolf, thirsty for Jewish blood. Because of that, he made no attempt to please the Jews. If Rome ever dealt with Jews using a velvet glove, it surely wasn't Pilate wearing it. Pilate answered not to the Roman Senate but to Tiberius himself. In the political system of that day, the governor answered to no one but the emperor. So in order for him to be removed, it took the emperor's edict.

Furthermore, Pilate was not a novice. For a man to become a governor, he had to come through the ranks. He had to be known as a brave Roman soldier. He had to be a leader. He had to be a hard administrator and a legislator. He had to be a man of decision.

And Pilate was no fool. The youngest Roman governor on record was twenty-seven years of age. Even if Pilate had been that young when he became governor, and we don't know that he was, then at this point he would have been the same age as Jesus—in his early thirties. However, it is much more likely that he was a man between forty and fifty. He was a hardened, cruel, seasoned Roman official.

This is much more in keeping with the Pilate described in a letter from Agrippa to Caligula, recorded in the writings of Philo. Caligula was the emperor after Tiberius, and this is the scathing testimony he received from Agrippa: "Pilate is unbending and recklessly hard. He is a man of notorious reputation, severe brutality, prejudice, savage violence, and murder."

As a result, Pilate was "on report," as we would say in military terms. He was under investigation by Rome. The emperor had ordered surveillance on this man, due to his suspicion after reading reports about the governor. An investigation was going on during the time Jesus was on trial. This explains why the otherwise unbending, brutal, prejudiced Pilate appears so vacillating and indecisive. This explains why he doesn't throw the Jews out of the palace when they come asking for the death of Jesus. Candidly, the man was scared. This hardened, Jew-hating Roman cared nothing about public opinion, except when his own neck was in the noose.

All of this seems confirmed by later history. Pilate was eventually banished by Caligula to Gaul, a distant region, far to the northwest of Italy, beyond the Alps. There, he suffered what sounds like an emotional or mental breakdown and, ultimately, committed suicide.

This was the man who would now decide the fate of the Son of God.

> Pilate asked Jesus, "Are you the king of the Jews?"
>
> Jesus answered, "Those are your words."
>
> The leading priests accused Jesus of many things. So Pilate asked Jesus another question, "You can see that they are accusing you of many things. Aren't you going to answer?"
>
> But Jesus still said nothing, so Pilate was very surprised.
>
> —MARK 15:2–5

"King" was the word that concerned Pilate. The charge of blasphemy meant nothing to him. But to a loyal Roman, Caesar was the only king—"We have no king but Caesar"—so anyone claiming to be king would be of enormous concern to Pilate, and even more so to Rome. Hence, the Jewish leaders accused Jesus of claiming to be "the King of the Jews."

> So Pilate asked them, "Do you want me to free the king of the Jews?" Pilate knew that the leading priests had turned Jesus in to him because they were jealous. But the leading priests had persuaded the people to ask Pilate to free Barabbas, not Jesus.
>
> Then Pilate asked the crowd again, "So what should I do with this man you call the king of the Jews?"
>
> They shouted, "Crucify him!"
>
> Pilate asked, "Why? What wrong has he done?"
>
> But they shouted even louder, "Crucify him!"
>
> —MARK 15:9–14

> Then the whole body of them got up and brought Him before Pilate. And they began to accuse Him, saying, "We found this man misleading our nation and forbidding to pay taxes to Caesar, and saying that He Himself is Christ, a King."
>
> And Pilate asked Him, saying, "Are You the King of the Jews?" And He answered him and said, "It is as you say."
>
> And Pilate said to the chief priests and the multitudes, "I find no guilt in this man."
>
> —LUKE 23:1–4, NASB

Obviously Pilate did not take this charge seriously. Being full of mischief himself, he saw through the chief priests' trumped-up charge. At most, Pilate viewed Jesus of Nazareth as another strange, self-appointed Messiah.

Though I am unable to state the source of his remark, I distinctly recall one of my professors at seminary telling us that many people claimed to be the Messiah. According to his research, several men in Jesus's day falsely claimed to be the Messiah of Israel. Should that have been so, Pilate would have been all the more skeptical. But false prophets and phony Messiahs were not the business of the Roman government or courts.

"You take care of this Jesus yourself," Pilate told the Jews with a cynical sneer and wave of his hand. "As far as I'm concerned, he's not guilty of anything."

But the Jewish leaders wouldn't give up:

> They were insisting, saying, "But Jesus makes trouble with the people, teaching all around Judea. He began in Galilee, and now he is here."
>
> —LUKE 23:5

Take the time to observe how John records this fourth trial. Read his words slowly and carefully.

> They led Jesus therefore from Caiaphas into the Praetorium, and it was early; and they themselves did not enter into the Praetorium in order that they might not be defiled, but might eat the Passover.
>
> Therefore Pilate went out to them, and said, "What accusation do you bring against this Man?"
>
> They answered and said to him, "If this Man were not an evildoer, we would not have delivered Him up to you."

So Pilate said to them, "Take Him yourselves, and judge Him according to your law." The Jews said to him, "We are not permitted to put anyone to death," to fulfill the word of Jesus, which He spoke, signifying by what kind of death He was about to die.

Therefore Pilate entered again into the Praetorium, and summoned Jesus, and said to Him, "Are You the King of the Jews?"

—John 18:28–33, NASB

Notice how legalistic the Jewish leaders were to keep themselves ceremonially pure: "They themselves did not enter into the Praetorium in order that they might not be defiled, but might eat the Passover." While guilty of false accusations, brutality, prejudice, and numerous illegal proceedings, the scrupulous hypocrites were careful to observe the proper religious boundaries at the Praetorium!

This is the same trial recorded in Luke 23, but John gives us more detail, particularly the interaction between Jesus and Pilate.

"Come on in here," Pilate says, in effect. "Let's get away from the crowd. Let's talk." So the two men go into the inner sanctum where Pilate presses Jesus, "Are You the King of the Jews?"

"Are you saying this on your own initiative," Jesus asks, "or did others tell you about Me?"

"I'm not a Jew, am I?" snaps Pilate. "Your own people turned You over to me. What have You done to offend them?"

Jesus answered, "My kingdom is not of this world. If I were truly leading an insurrection, don't you think my followers would be fighting in the streets?"

Then Pilate asks one of the most telling questions in this entire interrogation:

Pilate said, "So you are a king!"

Jesus answered, "You are the one saying I am a king. This is why I was born and came into the world: to tell people the truth. And everyone who belongs to the truth listens to me."

Pilate said, "What is truth?"

—JOHN 18:37–38

Here is a man who holds a position of authority as significant as the governor of Judea, yet he asks this stranger he has just met, "What is truth?" Such a question forces us to wonder upon what standards Pilate made his decisions or formed his judgments? Furthermore, can you imagine the man's level of confusion? He had no clue.

To look at his question less critically, we find ourselves at a loss to interpret why he asked it. Was he being facetious or scornful? Impatient or cynical? Despairing or sincere? Hard to tell. We're left to wonder. But while we may not know *that* answer, we do know that Pilate considered Jesus innocent of any crime. He may have seen him as a harmless philosopher or an impractical religious dreamer, but He certainly didn't qualify as a dangerous subversive. Initially, Pilate had the fortitude to stand against the swelling ranks of Jesus's accusers and announce, "I find nothing against this man" (John 18:38).

Pilate walks back out to the Jewish leaders and the mob and says, in effect, "I find no wrongdoing in this man. I've examined Him. We've talked. He's innocent."

But Pilate is in a tough spot himself. Every move he makes that raises their ire brings him under tighter scrutiny by Rome. Several riots have broken out in the streets of Jerusalem, and he does not want a fresh insurrection on his hands. He now fits the description of the weak politician who wants peace at any price. If he turns Jesus loose, these Jewish leaders might incite the mob to riot.

But Pilate's stubborn conscience says, "This man is not guilty." There's still enough anti-Semitism in him to keep him from giving these pompous Jews from the Temple what they want. So, searching for another out, he inadvertently finds one. It must have made him smile deep within. Watch what happens:

> They were insisting, saying, "But Jesus makes trouble with the people, teaching all around Judea. He began in Galilee, and now he is here."
> Pilate heard this and asked if Jesus was from Galilee. Since Jesus was under Herod's authority, Pilate sent Jesus to Herod, who was in Jerusalem at that time.
> —Luke 23:5–7

When Pilate heard "Galilee," he must have thought, "Aha! There's my loophole." Since this Jesus is a Galilean, that would place Him under Herod's jurisdiction, "and Herod's in town!"

In predictably political fashion, Pilate passes the buck and hopes someone else will make the tough call.

The Fifth Trial: Jesus Before Herod

Herod Antipas, who was tetrarch over Galilee from 4 BC to AD 39, was a member of the notorious Herod family. They were a brutal bunch, bone-deep cruel, capable of murdering their own spouses and siblings. I've often referred to them as "the godfathers of the ancient world"—deceitful and dangerous, powerful and controlling.

Herod and Jesus were not unknown to each other. This was the same Herod who had had John the Baptizer beheaded, the same Herod whom Jesus called "that fox" (Luke 13:32).

When Herod saw Jesus, he was very glad, because he had heard about Jesus and had wanted to meet him for a long time. He was hoping to see Jesus work a miracle. Herod asked Jesus many questions, but Jesus said nothing. The leading priests and teachers of the law were standing there, strongly accusing Jesus. After Herod and his soldiers had made fun of Jesus, they dressed him in a kingly robe and sent him back to Pilate. In the past, Pilate and Herod had always been enemies, but on that day they became friends.

—LUKE 23:8–12

The political ploy didn't work as Pilate had hoped. Herod Antipas, looking for cheap entertainment, starts firing questions. With His innocence established in His previous examination, Jesus takes a different defense tactic. He remains absolutely silent. Though Herod anticipates a show, he finds that Jesus is not an entertainer and is not given to satisfying idle curiosity. How disappointing for Herod! (And it will prove even more so for Pilate.)

Few authors do a better job of describing in a few words what transpired than Alexander Whyte:

> Herod Antipas was more of a circus-master than a serious-minded monarch; and, instead of taking up the case that had been referred to his jurisdiction, all that Herod aimed at was to get some amusement out of the accused. "He is the King of the Jews, is he? He is a candidate for my royal seat, is he? Then put the white coat of a candidate upon him and send him back to Pilate! The Governor will enjoy my jest; and it will somewhat cement our recovered friendship!"[1]

Herod, for some reason, was not in a killing mood but a playful one. He was hoping to see some kind of performance—a little miracle magic, perhaps. But nothing like that was forthcoming. Jesus refused to cooperate. Though questioned at length, the Nazarene remained mute before Herod.

So after staging his own little entertainment by dressing Jesus up in a kingly robe and mocking him, Herod shrugs the whole thing off and sends Him back to Pilate.

THE SIXTH TRIAL: JESUS BEFORE PILATE AGAIN

Pilate looks up from his breakfast and groans. *Oh, no.* He thought he had this nicely taken care of . . . out of his hands . . . off his plate . . . no longer his problem. Wrong. Now, what does he do?

Well, he's not yet out of ideas; so he tries another approach.

> Every year at the time of Passover the governor would free one prisoner whom the people chose. At that time there was a man in prison, named Barabbas, who was known to be very bad. When the people gathered at Pilate's house, Pilate said, "Whom do you want me to set free: Barabbas or Jesus who is called the Christ?" Pilate knew that the people turned Jesus in to him because they were jealous.
>
> While Pilate was sitting there on the judge's seat, his wife sent this message to him: "Don't do anything to that man, because he is innocent. Today I had a dream about him, and it troubled me very much."
>
> But the leading priests and older leaders convinced the crowd to ask for Barabbas to be freed and for Jesus to be killed.
>
> Pilate said, "I have Barabbas and Jesus. Which do you

want me to set free for you?"

The people answered, "Barabbas."

Pilate asked, "So what should I do with Jesus, the one called the Christ?"

They all answered, "Crucify him!"

Pilate asked, "Why? What wrong has he done?"

But they shouted louder, "Crucify him!"

When Pilate saw that he could do nothing about this and that a riot was starting, he took some water and washed his hands in front of the crowd. Then he said, "I am not guilty of this man's death. You are the ones who are causing it!"

All the people answered, "We and our children will be responsible for his death."

Then he set Barabbas free. But Jesus was beaten with whips and handed over to the soldiers to be crucified.

—MATTHEW 27:15–26

Keep in mind, up to this moment absolutely *nothing* has been proven against Jesus. He has not been proven guilty of anything. Each trial has had glaring illegalities. Not one reliable witness has spoken against Him. There is not a shred of damaging evidence proving guilt. Yet, strangely, He is still on trial.

At this point, Matthew informs us about a tradition of the time.

Although no other record of it can be found, there must have been the custom of releasing one prisoner at every Passover as a means of placating the Jewish population. Pilate seized on the opportunity to appeal to the masses and suggested that he would release Jesus if they demanded it. His proposal assumed that Jesus was popular with the general crowd, who did not always favor the hierarchy. . . . Pilate miscalculated the attitude of the crowd at this point.[2]

Once again Pilate thinks he may have a simple solution to his dilemma—another way out. He would offer them a choice between an innocent Galilean and the most notorious criminal they had imprisoned at the time, Barabbas. Barabbas was not only an insurrectionist, he was also a murderer, awaiting his own death by crucifixion.

I'm convinced that the center cross that day was intended for Barabbas, whom we will discuss further in the next chapter. Pilate "knew that the people turned Jesus in to him because they were jealous" (v. 18). Surely they would not carry this travesty any further. Surely they would rather have Jesus released than a man who had committed such heinous crimes, a man who was obviously dangerous. Brilliant idea, but again . . . wrong. "But the leading priests and older leaders convinced the crowd to ask for Barabbas to be freed and for Jesus to be killed" (v. 20).

Then Matthew introduces another character into this drama: Pilate's wife.

> While Pilate was sitting there on the judge's seat, his wife sent this message to him: "Don't do anything to that man, because he is innocent. Today I had a dream about him, and it troubled me very much."
>
> —MATTHEW 27:19

This is one of the most intriguing verses in the New Testament. Wouldn't you love to know what that dream was about? It must have really been vivid to prompt Pilate's wife to send him a note. Either Pilate had told her about his first encounter with Jesus while they were together, alone, the previous evening, or something in the dream had alerted her to what was going on. Now, along with all his other worries, he has this ominous warning to weigh into the equation.

"But the leading priests and older leaders convinced the crowd to ask for Barabbas to be freed and for Jesus to be killed" (v.20). Look who did that! The religious people. The religious *leaders!* Why? Because Barabbas was no threat to the religious phonies. He didn't hassle the legalists. He wasn't out there preaching in the streets. He was just engaged in mob violence and, occasionally, killing a few people.

"Let Him be crucified!" screamed the mob.

"Why, what evil has He done?" asks Pilate. "Show me the proof."

Do you know why they didn't answer? Because they *had* no answer. Jesus had done no evil. There was no proof of a crime. And so they screamed in their murderous, hateful frenzy, "Let Him be crucified! Let Him be crucified."

Pilate had reached the peak of pressure. He knew he had a riot on his hands and that "he could do nothing about this." And so he washed his hands of the whole affair. He caved in to the pressure. He looked the other way. Instead of standing firm and doing what was right, he compromised.

> When Pilate saw that he could do nothing about this and that a riot was starting, he took some water and washed his hands in front of the crowd. Then he said, "I am not guilty of this man's death. You are the ones who are causing it!"
>
> All the people answered, "We and our children will be responsible for his death."
>
> Then he set Barabbas free. But Jesus was beaten with whips and handed over to the soldiers to be crucified.
>
> MATTHEW 27:24–26

With the ending of the sixth and final trial, rationalization goes on parade. Pilate goes through this ceremonial moment, saying verbally and symbolically, "I'm cleansing myself of all responsibility for this travesty of justice."

It says a lot that this man, known for his cruelty as a ruler, suffers pangs of conscience over Jesus's trial—so much so that he acquits himself before the Jews, whom he hated as much as he hated anything, and whom he knows have framed this innocent Man. No boldness or arrogance here, which is what you might expect of Pilate in this setting, before this audience. Instead he shows the weakness of conscience and a total absence of character.

In so doing, Pilate sends an innocent man to the cross and, consequently, spares a guilty one from his.

✝

*But he took our suffering on him
and felt our pain for us.*

ISAIAH 53:4

5

THE Man WHO Missed His Cross

HEADLINE FROM THE *Jerusalem Post:*

INSURRECTIONIST AND CONVICTED MURDERER PARDONED MINUTES BEFORE HIS CRUCIFIXION.

Mystery surrounds the man who took his place. Some say he was a treasonous zealot, some say a harmless Jewish preacher, others a miracle worker. Rumor has it, the Roman governor of Judea, Pilate, said he was absolutely innocent. . . ."

IF CNN HAD BEEN THERE ON THAT DAY, people around the world would have awakened to such sensational headlines. As we examined at the end of the previous chapter, an ironic twist of perverted justice takes place—an innocent man receives the cross of a guilty man. Of all people, Barabbas, only minutes away from his execution, got his get-out-of-jail-free card.

Having been convicted and condemned to die, his cell is most likely located in the fortress of Antonia in the city of Jerusalem. From there Barabbas could hear the crowd crying for Jesus's blood. He can't decipher every word and nuance, but he can hear the mob shouting at the top of their lungs, in their frenzy to intimidate Pilate.

"Barabbas! Barabbas. Give us Barabbas!" they scream.

Barabbas hears his name. The next thing he hears chills him to the bone: "Crucify him!" He now knows one thing for sure: He will soon be on his way to the cross.

In his mind, he pictures his own horrifying death by crucifixion. That will be the end of the trail, and a torturous end at that. No need to go beyond the driving of the nails into his flesh. Hopefully, death will come soon. All who hung on crosses hoped for quick deaths.

But for Barabbas, life didn't end on a cross. The jailer who opened his cell didn't march him to his execution. He set him free!

Wouldn't you love to know what happened to Barabbas after he was freed? After he learned that an innocent Man had died in his place? Wouldn't you like to know what he did with the rest of his life?

Did he continue in his evil ways, yet escape any earthly punishment? Was he arrested after another crime or, perhaps, killed in the process? Or did he come to worship the One who had died in his place? Was he, as some legends maintain, standing among the crowd at the foot of the cross, watching Jesus die?

If asked to describe Barabbas, all of us could do it in one sentence: He was the man released in place of Jesus. But there is more to the story, much more.

To appreciate that story, we need to understand some things about the culture and tradition of Jesus's day. According to Matthew's and Mark's accounts, during Passover the governor normally released any prisoner the people wanted. Though no one seems to be able to explain how the custom began, it was clearly in place at the time of Jesus's trials.

> Every year at the time of Passover the governor would free
> one prisoner whom the people chose.
> —MATTHEW 27:15

Every year at the time of the Passover the governor would free one prisoner whom the people chose. At that time, there was a man named Barabbas in prison who was a rebel and had committed murder during a riot. The crowd came to Pilate and began to ask him to free a prisoner as he always did.

—MARK 15:6–8

Apparently the Jewish people would approach the governor and say, "At this Passover time, we request that you release Aristobulus." And regardless of what he had done, or what he was accused of, Aristobulus would be released from prison, scot-free.

Most of the time, no doubt, that custom was a thorn in the flesh to Pilate, the anti-Semitic, brutal governor of Judea. But this time he welcomed the custom with a sigh of relief. We looked at Pilate in depth in the previous chapter, which helps us understand that he was a man balancing his career on the horns of a dilemma.

First of all, he was scared. He knew that the Jewish leaders had trumped up the charge against Jesus because they were jealous of His power over the people. But Pilate also knew that if he did not cooperate with them, they would riot. Should another bad report about his regime go back to Rome, Pilate was sure he would lose his position as governor.

His second dilemma was that he was convinced that Jesus was innocent. Of all the judges Jesus stood before in those final hours of trial, Pilate was the only one who gave Him half a chance to declare His innocence. Pilate looked for the facts, and when he found them he was not hesitant to say, "He's innocent!" When the Jews would not accept that verdict, Pilate found himself afraid to condemn this innocent Man, so he washed his hands of the matter and allowed Jesus to be crucified.

British scholar James Stalker, who has written a fine volume on

Jesus's trials and death, puts it succinctly. Referring to Pilate's choice of Barabbas, he writes, "What he had considered a loophole of escape was a noose into which he had thrust his head."[1]

But the question remains: Why, of all the prisoners sitting in Roman cells, did Pilate select Barabbas? Why not one of the two thieves scheduled to be crucified that day—the two later crucified alongside Jesus? Why would Pilate offer to free a man with the kind of notorious criminal record that Barabbas had?

His Name

> At that time they were holding a notorious prisoner called Barabbas.
>
> —MATTHEW 27:16, NASB

The word translated "notorious" comes from a term that means "to mark upon." Based on the meaning of the Greek word, Barabbas was a marked man. In our terms, he was "public enemy number one." He was more than simply a rabble-rouser—more than another insurrectionist fomenting unrest throughout Judea. He was no petty thief, picking pockets in the crowded streets of Jerusalem. Barabbas was a murderer, a hardened killer.

His name itself is significant. Notice that he is called "Bar-abbas," an Aramaic name. Aramaic was the spoken language of that day, the language spoken by Jesus and His disciples. But Barabbas was not a common Aramaic name.

As you can see, it divides easily into "Bar" and "abbas." When Jesus addressed Peter on one occasion, He called him "Simon Barjona." Simon was his given name, Barjona was his received name. Our received name is our last name. My children possess given names as their first names, but their last name is Swindoll, the same as mine.

Swindoll is their received name. In biblical days, children also received their father's name. "Bar" means "son," so Simon Barjona means, "Simon, son of John."

We are not told Barabbas's given name. We are told only his received name: Bar-abbas, meaning "son of abbas." And here's the intriguing part of it: "Abbas, or "abba" means "Father." So Bar-abbas would mean "son of the father." But that doesn't help much. Obviously any man is the son of his father. But there's more. Commentator William Barclay notes that the name "may be compounded of Bar-Rabban, which would mean 'son of the Rabbi.'"[2] Thus, this could mean that Bar-abbas was the son of a well-known rabbi, or at least a well-known teacher. If that were the case, his criminal activities would have been both notorious and scandalous.

This is more than mere legend or supposition. The Jewish historian Josephus agrees with Matthew, stating that Barabbas was a notorious criminal *before* he was caught. Possibly this was not only because of his heinous crimes but also because of the well-known family from which he came.

> When the people gathered at Pilate's house, Pilate said, "Whom do you want me to set free: Barabbas or Jesus who is called the Christ?" Pilate knew that the people turned Jesus in to him because they were jealous.
>
> But the leading priests and older leaders convinced the crowd to ask for Barabbas to be freed and for Jesus to be killed.
>
> Pilate said, "I have Barabbas and Jesus. Which do you want me to set free for you?"
>
> The people answered, "Barabbas."
>
> Pilate asked, "So what should I do with Jesus, the one called the Christ?"

They all answered, "Crucify him!"
—Matthew 27:17–18,20–22

In these verses Pilate refers to Jesus as "Jesus who is called Christ." It almost seems as if he is distinguishing Him from some other Jesus. Indeed, I suggest he is. According to some of the most ancient manuscripts of Matthew, two of them in particular, the gospel writer notes that Barabbas's first or given name was Yeshua (Jesus), which explains why Pilate would say, "Whom shall I release? Yeshua Barabbas or Yeshua Christ?"

Now the logical question: Why doesn't this name appear in our Bibles today?

Dr. William Riley Wilson, a keen New Testament scholar, notes this concerning the omission of Barabbas's first name. "It seems very unlikely that any Christian scribes could accidentally have included Jesus's name at this point in the text, but it is easy to see why Christian copyists would intentionally have deleted the name Jesus as a designation for the murderous Barabbas."[3]

When these texts were copied by hand, the scribes would have been careful to note when they came to the full name of Jesus, such as "Jesus, who is called the Anointed One." But when they came to the name of the murderer Barabbas, naturally they would not want to attach "Yeshua" to his name. That is Wilson's point.

"The name Jesus . . . was a common one in first-century Judea, much like James or John today. It is quite possible that Barabbas bore this name. But since the name Jesus was especially sacred to the early Church, it would have been most natural for the early Christians to dissociate it from the murderer Barabbas. This would have been accomplished by gradually omitting Barabbas's given name from the oral and written records of the trial. If this suggestion is correct, the few manuscripts which give the name Jesus Barabbas are the only surviving evidence of the insurrectionist's full name."[4]

This makes Pilate's choice of Barabbas logical. His thinking probably went something like this: "Here is a man with a given name identical to that of Jesus of Nazareth. Surely they will not want the murderer released. Surely they'd rather have the Jesus who claims to be their Messiah." Unfortunately, Pilate's plan backfired. As Stalker stated: His hope for a loophole became his noose.

HIS CRIME

Now at the feast he used to release for them any one prisoner whom they requested.

The man named Barabbas had been imprisoned with the insurrectionists who had committed murder in the insurrection.

—MARK 15:6–7, NASB

Mark sheds even more light on the situation. (Often it is helpful to compare one gospel writer with another. Different narrators assist us in getting a clearer picture. We benefit from comparing the testimonies of the four writers). The record from Mark's account states, "Barabbas had been imprisoned with the insurrectionists," which verifies that the two men who were later crucified with Jesus were fellow insurrectionists with Barabbas.

Barabbas had been arrested and convicted of insurrection and murder. Insurrection is a one-word description of rebellion against the ruling authorities.

Barabbas was no petty pilferer or "sneak thief," writes William Barclay in his Daily Study Bible Series. "He was a brigand or a political revolutionary." There must have been a rough audacity about him that would appeal to the crowd. Palestine, you see, was filled with rebellions. It was an inflammable land. In particular there was one group of Jews called the Sicarri, which means dagger-bearers. They were violent, fanatical zealots. They were pledged to murder and assassination by any possible means. They carried daggers beneath their cloaks, and they used them as they could. It is very likely that Barabbas was such a man.[5]

Barabbas, the criminal whom Governor Pilate offered to the Jews in his prisoner-release program, was a dangerous rebel, a man of violence and murder. Our description today would be "terrorist."

HIS LOCATION

All four of the gospel writers—Matthew, Mark, Luke, and John—state or imply that Barabbas was imprisoned or bound by the Roman authorities.

> And they were holding at that time a notorious prisoner, called Barabbas.
> —MATTHEW 27:16, NASB

> And the man named Barabbas had been imprisoned with the insurrectionists who had committed murder in the insurrection.
> —MARK 15:7, NASB

> But the people shouted together, "Take this man away! Let Barabbas go free!"
> —LUKE 23:18

But it is your custom that I free one prisoner to you at Passover time. Do you want me to free the 'king of the Jews'?"

They shouted back, "No, not him! Let Barabbas go free!" (Barabbas was a robber.)

—JOHN 18:39–40

As mentioned earlier, Barabbas was probably imprisoned at the fortress of Antonia, the "holding tank" for most prisoners in ancient Jerusalem. During Passover that city was a crowded, noisy place. The narrow streets were packed with Jews from many countries, since Jerusalem was the place to be at Passover time. The criminal element was evident as well, including various zealots rebelling against Rome, which is why Pilate had left his palatial headquarters in the beautiful, blue Mediterranean coastal city of Caesarea. He came to Jerusalem to maintain law and order. With Pilate came a battalion of Roman soldiers, who were stationed at the barracks in the fortress of Antonia—the same stone building where Barabbas was held captive.

But where was Pilate? He could have been staying at the Hasmonian Palace. However, that was the residence of Herod Antipas when he was in Jerusalem (according to several historians), and Herod "was in Jerusalem at that time" (Luke 23:7). That suggests Pilate stayed in safe quarters at the fortress of Antonia, a Roman fortress and the headquarters for the Roman soldiers in the area.

THE PAVEMENT

As a result of this Pilate made efforts to release Him, but the Jews cried out, saying, "If you release this Man, you are no friend of Caesar; everyone who makes himself out to be a king opposes Caesar."

When Pilate therefore heard these words, he brought Jesus out, and sat down on the judgment seat at a place called The Pavement, but in Hebrew, Gabbatha.

—John 19:12–13, NASB

At this sixth and final trial of Jesus, Pilate paraded Jesus out to a place called "The Pavement." In Hebrew it is *Gabbatha,* which means "mosaic, or stone." This was an elevated area, paved with stone or hand-laid tiles, in a courtyard just outside the palace or the fortress, where Pilate sat to pass judgments, hear cases, or dispense other rulings. It was here that Pilate brought Jesus to interview Him and, finally, to present Him to the waiting mob. Remember, the Jewish leaders wouldn't go into Pilate's residence, because they didn't want to defile themselves at Passover time.

Now, where was this place located in relationship to where Barabbas was incarcerated? What was the distance between them?

The distance between the fortress and the palace was about two thousand feet, a little less than half a mile. From that distance, Barabbas could certainly hear from his cell the noise of the angry mob. Keeping that in mind, the story gets very interesting.

Picture Barabbas, imprisoned in a dark dungeon in the fortress of Antonia, awaiting execution. As suggested earlier, the third cross was intended for Barabbas. He was awaiting execution that very day.

Barabbas paces his cell . . . anxious . . . afraid. Suddenly, he hears the sound of an angry mob in the distance. Did that mean his fellow zealots were rioting? Were they, perhaps, overthrowing the Roman guards and coming to his rescue? In his situation, he would hope so.

Suddenly, he hears his name. "Barabbas . . . Barabbas!"

Pilate said, "I have Barabbas and Jesus. Which do you want me to set free for you?"

—MATTHEW 27:21

But the people shouted together, "Take this man away! Let Barabbas go free!"

—LUKE 23:18

They shouted back, "No, not him! Let Barabbas go free!" (Barabbas was a robber.)

—JOHN 18:40

From half a mile away Barabbas could hear the mob shouting his name. And what did he hear next? Check the record, according to Matthew:

Pilate said, "I have Barabbas and Jesus. Which do you want me to set free for you?"

The people answered, "Barabbas."

Pilate asked, "So what should I do with Jesus, the one called the Christ?"

They all answered, "Crucify him!"

—MATTHEW 27:21–22

Barabbas's heart begins to pound. He knows this is no mob of zealous Jews coming to rescue him. This is a lynching party. Worse than that, a crucifixion party. He couldn't hear Pilate's lone voice asking the questions. All he could hear were the frenzied cries of the mob. "Barabbas!" . . . followed by, "Crucify him!"

Suddenly he hears the measured tread, the deliberate slap of leather against stone pavement. Soldiers marching down the stone stairway, coming toward his cell. Closer . . . closer they come. One of them swings wide the iron door and growls, "Get out of here, Barabbas." His heart sinks. But then he hears, "You're free to go."

Can you imagine his shock?

Barabbas, fully expecting the soldiers to come and take him to be crucified, suddenly finds himself a free man!

Seeing His Substitute

Barabbas was supposed to die that very day. He was guilty, sentenced, and imprisoned, awaiting his own death by crucifixion. Yet suddenly he was told, "You're free."

A number of legends have grown up around the character of Barabbas. They are just legends, and yet . . . a little imagination never hurts. And I have my own ideas on the subject.

I like to think that Barabbas stayed in Jerusalem that day. After all, he'd been freed. Instead of fleeing for the hills or seeking out his cronies in some back alley, he huddled in the background outside the city gate, anxious to see the Man who was nailed to the cross Barabbas himself deserved.

†

He was beaten down and punished,
but he didn't say a word.
He was like a lamb being led to be killed.
He was quiet, as a sheep is quiet
while its wool is being cut;
he never opened his mouth.

ISAIAH 53:7

6

THE WAY OF THE CROSS

SIR WINSTON CHURCHILL was not a man who drifted aimlessly through life. Those who knew him well and those of us who love to read his works know that he was consumed by compelling convictions of providence. His life became, to him, an unfolding sense of personal, even heroic destiny. I am not the first to suggest that leading his nation against the forces of Nazism and championing the cause of freedom, in spite of overwhelming odds, became his magnificent obsession.

When King George VI invited him, on May 10, 1940, to lead his beloved Britain against the enemy that threatened Europe, Churchill confidently accepted the challenge. As he later recounted, "I felt as if I were walking with destiny, and that all my past life had been but a preparation for this hour and for this trial."[1]

Jesus of Nazareth, too, had a magnificent obsession: the cross. Painful and anguishing though it was, He found Himself consumed by a compelling sense of Divine providence, and each day of His adult life drew Him inexorably closer to the fulfillment of that mission.

Jesus was not a helpless victim of fate, nor was He a pitiful martyr. Books have been written with that very plot in mind: that Jesus had devised a plan that failed and, when the tables turned on Him, wound up on a cross, but, happily, in the process, He established a new religion. Allow me to set the record straight: Jesus's death was a necessary part—in fact, the very core—of God's predetermined plan. His death on the cross was no afterthought on God's part but, rather, the fulfillment of the Father's plan for His Son.

In our imagination we are going to be walking where Jesus walked on His final journey to the cross. The path is not pleasant, but it is real. We need to revisit the scene, if we hope to gain a realistic understanding of what He endured.

DELIVERED TO BE CRUCIFIED

> When Pilate therefore heard these words, he brought Jesus out, and sat down on the judgment seat at a place called The Pavement, but in Hebrew, *Gabbatha*.
>
> Now it was the day of preparation for the Passover; it was about the sixth hour. And he said to the Jews, "Behold, your King!"
>
> They therefore cried out, "Away with Him, away with Him, crucify Him!" Pilate said to them, "Shall I crucify your King?" The chief priests answered, "We have no king but Caesar."
>
> So he then delivered Him to them to be crucified.
> —JOHN 19:13–16, NASB

As we saw in chapter 5, Pilate has washed his hands of the whole mess. He pronounced the final sentence, turning Jesus over to the mob. Though knowing in his heart that Jesus was innocent, Pilate compromised his better judgment in order to appease the people.

The sixth and final trial took place around 7:30 in the morning.

Jesus's painful walk to Golgatha probably began shortly thereafter. The writings of Mark tell us that Jesus's hands and feet were nailed to the cross at 9:00 in the morning; so the torturous preliminaries occurred an hour, or an hour and a half, before that.

Physical Torture: Scourging

Then he released Barabbas for them; but after having Jesus scourged, he handed Him over to be crucified.
—Matthew 27:26, NASB

In those days there were two kinds of scourging or flogging: Jewish and Roman. The Jewish method is described in Deuteronomy 25:1–3, where we are told that a person was not to be beaten more than forty times. Because a Jew was afraid of breaking that law of God, he would commonly strike the victim thirty-nine times, making sure he counted meticulously so that he didn't go beyond forty. But in Roman scourging there was no specified number of times that a victim could be struck. Understandably, then, the Romans called their torturous act of scourging "halfway death."

Before the scourging began, the victim was stripped of all his clothing and bent forward over a low, thick stump or post. At the base of the post were four metal rings. The wrists and ankles of the victim were shackled to these rings. Jesus was stripped of His garments, bent low over this post, with His wrists and ankles secured.

The scourging was done by a man called a lictor—a professional in the grim task of torture. The instrument used for scourging was called a flagellum. It was a piece of wood fourteen to eighteen inches long, circular in shape (like a broom handle), to which were attached long, leather thongs. Into these leather thongs were sewn bits of glass, bone, and sharp pieces of metal.

The soldier who performed flagellations . . . moved to a position about six feet behind Jesus, and spread his legs. The flagellum was brought all the way back and whistled forward, making a dull drum sound as the strips of leather smashed against the back of the rib cage. The bits of bone and chain curled around the right side of the body and raised small subcutaneous hemorrhages on the chest . . .

The flagellum came back again, aimed slightly lower, and again, aimed higher, and it crashed against skin and flesh. . . . The flagellum now moved in slow heavy rhythm.[2]

It was designed to reduce the naked body to strips of raw flesh and inflamed, bleeding wounds.

It was not uncommon for victims to die on the stump. As the New International Version of the Bible notes: "Roman floggings were so brutal that sometimes the victim died before crucifixion." [See NIV footnote on Matthew 27:26.] Invariably, the one being beaten passed out from pain, only to be revived by being splashed with buckets of salt water. These torturers layered pain upon pain to keep the victim conscious, wanting him to suffer as much as possible. The one in charge of this torture kept watch. It was his responsibility to stop the "discipline" if he thought the guilty one might not be revived.

PUBLIC HUMILIATION: MOCKERY AND BRUTALITY

The governor's soldiers took Jesus into the governor's palace, and they all gathered around him. They took off his clothes and put a red robe on him. Using thorny branches, they made a crown, put it on his head, and put a stick in his right hand. Then the soldiers bowed before Jesus and made fun of him, saying, "Hail, King of the

Jews!." They spat on Jesus. Then they took his stick and
began to beat him on the head.

—MATTHEW 27:27–30

At this point Jesus became a comic figure to the Roman soldiers.
Silent, He stood before them as they began to humiliate, degrade, and
mock Him in every possible way.

The first thing the soldiers did was strip Jesus of all His clothing.
He stood nude before them, His face and body a mass of swollen and
bruised flesh. Then, in sarcastic fashion, they jammed a crown on His
head—a crown they had fashioned from thorns. They draped a red
robe over Him and placed a stick in His hand to represent a royal
scepter. They mocked Him cruelly, bowing down before Him and
hailing Him loudly as "King of the Jews!"

The Greek word Matthew uses when referring to the robe is
chlamus. It is not the word for a long flowing robe; rather, it was a
short cloak that came only to the elbows. It was spread over the shoulders and was probably fastened with some kind of tie or button at the
neck. In other words, the Son of God stood there naked from His
waist down before that barracks full of crude, godless men. In fact,
I'm confident that is why we do not have a record of what they said
to Him. Having spent time in a military barracks, I have some idea
of the kind of language they would have used. You can believe that as
Jesus stood in that humiliating place in front of those uncaring men,
He heard every obscene and coarse comment aimed at Him, yet "he
never opened his mouth" (Isaiah 53:7).

The reference to a "crown of thorns" is equally intriguing. Thorns
were common in that area. The longer ones were snipped, stuffed in a
basket or pot, dried, and then used as kindling to start fires. Outside,
in public places there would be large receptacles stocked with these
dried thorns and vines. Probably the soldiers went out, snatched a few

thorn branches from the container, plaited together a crown, and, with sneers and vulgar jesting, shoved it down on His head.

Several years ago, when friends of mine were in Jerusalem, they found a fairly authentic replica of what that crown probably looked like. Some of the thorns are three and a half inches long. These sharp thorns would have torn cruelly into Jesus's scalp and forehead.

"Hail, King of the Jews!" the Romans shouted. How they hated the Jews! In their brutal mockery, they vented all of their rage on this innocent Man. But their hateful abuse took shape in more than costuming and words: They spit on Him and beat Him on the head with the stick scepter. Anyone who has seen Mel Gibson's film *The Passion of the Christ* has witnessed as realistic an enactment of this torturous procedure as anything ever written or filmed before.

Jesus was mocked, brutalized, and mistreated for an extended period of time before He was led to the place of execution. Quite likely in shock from the extensive physical trauma He had endured, He no doubt began to shake and shiver following all the blows. His face became so marked and swollen that His individual features were no longer distinguishable. Prior to His walk to Golgotha, He was brought back before Pilate and the bloodthirsty mob.

"Behold, the Man!"

Pilate made his announcement, pointing to Jesus while facing the mob.

"Crucify him!" they screamed in reply. Pilate stared in disbelief.

> After they finished, the soldiers took off the robe and put his own clothes on him again. Then they led him away to be crucified.
>
> —MATTHEW 27:31

Notice that before the soldiers took Jesus to the site of execution, they redressed Him—they "put His clothes on Him." In those days, the Jewish man traditionally wore five pieces of clothing: sandals on his feet, a headpiece called a turban, an inner tunic, an outer cloak, and a girdle (what we would call a wide belt).

After the condemned criminal was executed, these clothes would be divided among the soldiers.

GOING TO GOLGOTHA

Crucifixion was a common sight for those who lived under the domination of Rome. Perhaps that is why the gospel writers give us few details about Jesus's final walk to the site of execution.

Matthew simply says that the soldiers "led Him away to be crucified." Mark records that "they led him out to crucify him" (Mark 15:20). Luke tells us that "they led him away"(Luke 23:26). And John writes, "Carrying his own cross, Jesus went out to a place called The Place of the Skull, which in the Jewish language is called Golgotha." (John 19:17).

Matthew, Mark, and Luke, however, do give us one interesting detail.

> As the soldiers were going out of the city with Jesus, they forced a man from Cyrene, named Simon, to carry the cross for Jesus.
>
> —MATTHEW 27:32

> A man named Simon from Cyrene, the father of Alexander and Rufus, was coming from the fields to the city. The soldiers forced Simon to carry the cross for Jesus.
>
> —MARK 15:21

As they led Jesus away, Simon, a man from Cyrene, was coming in from the fields. They forced him to carry Jesus' cross and to walk behind him.

—LUKE 23:26

Once again let me remind you that crucifixion was a public event. The criminal was paraded from prison to his place of execution. The Romans wanted as many people as possible to see their "justice." Thus, following an established pattern, Jesus would have been paraded through the streets of Jerusalem to the execution site outside the city gate—a place where people were constantly coming and going. With a centurion in the lead and two soldiers on either side of Him, there was no possibility of escape, even if the victim had any physical endurance left or any friends who wanted to mount a last-minute rescue. The Romans, along with their pomp and sordid ritual for effect, were also taking no chances, especially with the Jewish zealots and insurrectionists who were capable of anything.

Many artists have painted pictures of Jesus carrying a huge cross on His back, bowed low beneath its weight. Certainly there is no way to measure the weight of the burden Jesus carried to the cross—the weight of our sin—or the degree of His suffering. However, in strictly physical terms, He could not have carried the two heavy timbers that formed the entire cross. The eight-foot, six-by-six-inch piece of rugged timber, plus a crossbeam of similar dimensions, would have been too heavy. The upright beam of the cross either remained at the execution site or was taken there by Roman soldiers ahead of time.

The victim did, however, carry the crossbeam of his own cross, which was burden enough. The beam was hoisted across his shoulders and chained to him. Then around his neck was hung a board, about twelve by twenty-four inches, on which was written a notice proclaiming his crime. That board would later be nailed above him on the cross so that all who passed by would know the crime for which he was being executed.

Beaten, bruised, and bleeding, Jesus staggered through the longest walk of His life. Through the narrow streets of Jerusalem crowded with the pilgrims there for Passover, who were buying and selling in the last few hours before all trading ceased at the beginning of *Shabbat* (the Sabbath), the soldiers led Jesus out to be crucified. Jesus's final walk to the cross is often called the *Via Dolorosa,* "the way of sorrow." While that is a hauntingly beautiful term (which has resulted in a lovely musical composition), there was nothing beautiful about Jesus's stumbling, halting, painful journey to the place of execution.

Jesus had been tortured and beaten so badly that He stumbled under the weight of the crossbeam, unable to go on—the beam too heavy for Him to carry. Mercifully, a man from the crowd was commandeered to help Him carry the beam. Simon of Cyrene, an otherwise obscure man from Africa, will forever be immortalized as the man who helped Jesus bear the weight of the beam, but no one could ever help Him bear the weight of His cross.

✝

*He willingly gave his life and
was treated like a criminal.*

ISAIAH 53:12

7

The Darkest of All Days

I was raised and now live in the State of Texas where, until recently, convicted murderers were executed in the electric chair. Other places use the gas chamber and, as they now do in Texas, lethal injection; and a few still use the firing squad and the hangman's noose. None of these methods of execution is pleasant or attractive, nor are they meant to be. Execution is the ultimate punishment for the ultimate crime: giving up one's own life for the deliberate act of taking the life of another person.

There is no way to make an instrument of death appealing; yet there is no doubt that some are much worse than others. Crucifixion ranks right up there on the short list of the most painful and torturous deaths ever devised.

Crucifixion differs in two major ways from the various forms of execution today.

First, today's executions are, for the most part, private events. They are private in the sense that the death itself is not viewed by the general public. At the time of execution a few are allowed to be witnesses, demonstrators may gather outside the prison, and those who demonstrate may be televised, if the execution has become notorious for some reason, but cameras are not allowed at the execution itself. In contrast, crucifixion was not only allowed to be a public event, it was designed to be unforgettable for those who witnessed it. The Romans wanted their citizens to have a vivid reminder that the penalty for breaking their laws was certain, brutal, and extreme.

Crucifixion actually predates the Romans by several hundred years. According to journalist Jim Bishop, the inventors of this macabre method of execution designed crucifixion as a way to inflict the maximum amount of pain on a victim before death.

> They had tried death by spear, by boiling in oil, impalement, stoning, strangulation, drowning, burning—and all had been found to be too quick. They wanted a means of punishing criminals slowly and inexorably, so man devised the cross. It was almost ideal, because in its original form it was as slow as it was painful . . . and the condemned at the same time were placed fairly before the gaze of the people.
>
> A secondary consideration was nudity. This added to the shame of the evildoer and, at the same time, made him helpless before the thousands of insects in the air . . .
>
> The Romans adopted the cross as a means of deterring crime, and they had faith in it. In time they reduced it to an exact science with a set of rules to be followed.[1]

Second, today's executions are swift and even somewhat merciful: the sudden snap of a spine, the firing of a bullet through a heart, the gradual sleep brought on by noxious gas, the quiet, swift death of a lethal injection. Crucifixion was designed to be an excruciatingly painful, humiliating, and especially a lingering death. Merrill F. Unger, the late biblical scholar, states that "instances are on record of persons surviving for nine days"[2] on a cross.

Today the cross is an object of veneration. Designed into exquisite jewelry and artistic statuary, the cross has become a thing of beauty. The outline of the cross is set into mosaic tiles and highlighted with indirect lighting, framed in metal and etched in lovely, mood-setting stained glass. People of the first century would be shocked to see our modern treatment of what was, to them, an object of brutality and the cruelest kind of death. It would be comparable to our wearing the image of a hangman's noose on our lapel or framing an artist's rendering of a syringe with a long needle on our living room wall. In the first century the cross meant death . . . but not just any death. It meant the most hideous, torturous death imaginable.

DEATH BY CRUCIFIXION

A British scholar calls crucifixion "the dreadful routine." Klausner, a Jewish historian, says, "Crucifixion is the most terrible and cruel death man has ever devised." Cicero, who was well acquainted with it, says, "It was the most cruel and shameful of all punishments." William Wilson, in his judicial, literary, and historical investigation of what he calls "Jesus's execution," writes, "Not only was the cross the most painful of deaths, it was also considered the most debasing. The condemned man was stripped naked and left exposed in his agony, and often the Romans even denied burial to the victim, allowing his body to hang on the cross until it disintegrated."[3]

Centuries before Christ endured the horror of crucifixion, the Persians were sending men to their deaths on crosses. The Persians worshiped Ormuzd, the god of earth; therefore, they believed that no criminal's blood should contaminate the earth by the victim's dying on it. To avoid this, they devised an ingenious plan whereby a victim could be lifted off the "pure" earth and die in that position; the body could then be removed without ever touching the earth, thus keeping the earth pure. This method of execution was passed on to the Egyptians and ultimately to the Romans, who embraced it and refined it further.

I am indebted to Jim Bishop for the following vivid and lengthy description of crucifixion in Jesus's day:

> The executioner laid the crossbeam behind Jesus and brought him to the ground quickly by grasping his arm and pulling him backward. As soon as Jesus fell, the beam was fitted under the back of his neck and, on each side, soldiers quickly knelt on the inside of the elbows . . .
>
> Once begun, the matter was done quickly and efficiently. The executioner wore an apron with pockets. He placed two five-inch nails between his teeth and, hammer in hand, knelt beside the right arm. The soldier whose knee rested on the inside of the elbow held the forearm flat to the board. With his right hand the executioner probed the wrist of Jesus to find the little hollow spot [where there would be no vital artery or vein]. When he found it, he took one of the square-cut iron nails from his teeth and held it against the spot, directly behind where the so-called lifeline ends. Then he raised the hammer over the nail head and brought it down with force . . .
>
> The executioner jumps across the body to the other wrist . . .
>
> As soon as he was satisfied that the condemned man could not, in struggling, pull himself loose and perhaps fall forward off the cross, he brought both of his arms upward rapidly. This was the signal to lift the crossbeam.
>
> Two soldiers grabbed each side of the crossbeam and lifted. As they pulled up, they dragged Jesus by the wrists

. . . When the soldiers reached the upright, the four of them began to lift the crossbeam higher until the feet of Jesus were off the ground. The body must have writhed with pain . . .

When the crossbeam was set firmly, the executioner reached up, set the board which listed the name of the prisoner and the crime. Then he knelt before the cross. Two soldiers hurried to help, and each one took hold of a leg at the calf. The ritual was to nail the right foot over the left, and this was probably the most difficult part of the work. If the feet were pulled downward, and nailed close to the foot of the cross, the prisoner always died quickly. Over the years, the Romans learned to push the feet upward on the cross, so that the condemned man could lean on the nails so as to stretch himself upward.[4]

Some historians describe a saddle-like piece of wood fixed to the vertical post, where the victim could rest the base of his pelvis in order to find momentary relief.

With his arms now in a V position, Jesus became conscious of two unendurable circumstances: The first was that the pain in His wrists was beyond bearing, causing muscle cramps that knotted His forearms and upper arms and the pads of His shoulders. The second was that His pectoral muscles along both sides of His chest were momentarily paralyzed. This induced in Him an involuntary panic; for He found that while he could draw air into his lungs, He was powerless to exhale.

To be able to keep breathing, the victim on the cross had to remain in constant motion. He literally dragged himself up and down, up and down, monotonously and continually, so as to make breathing possible. Eventually, he could no longer lift himself sufficiently to continue breathing.

With each second, the pain mounted. His arms, His legs, His entire torso screamed with pain; the nerves were pulled tightly, like strings of a violin across its bridge. Slowly and steadily, he was being asphyxiated, as though two thumbs were pressing against His throat.

Some suggest that victims of crucifixion died of suffocation. Others teach that they died from hunger. Still others maintain that they died from sheer exhaustion, as the body eventually wore out from the unendurable pain and the unnatural suspension of the organs and muscles.

As Harvie Branscomb summarizes:

> Few more terrible means of execution could be devised. Pain, thirst, the torture of insects, exposure to brutal spectators, the horror of rigid fixation, all continuing interminably, combined to make it a supreme humiliation and torture.[5]

The Path Ends

> It was about noon, and the whole land became dark until three o' clock in the afternoon, because the sun did not shine. The curtain in the Temple was torn in two. Jesus cried out in a loud voice, "Father, I give you may life." After Jesus said this, he died.
>
> —Luke 23:44–46

He hung on the cross for six hours, each breath moving Him closer to death. Now we understand why He had prayed in Gethsemane for His "cup to pass." Betrayed and abandoned by friends, falsely accused, publicly humiliated, beaten beyond recognition, thorns dug into His brow, and crucified as a common criminal, Jesus endured pain beyond our comprehension. And yet, we know He accepted this path from the beginning. He was born to die. The shadow of the cross followed Him from womb to tomb.

✝

Behold . . . the Man.

Take a long look at Him. He has come a long way from Bethlehem's manger. From a wooden trough to a wooden stake. You can't help but stare at Him hanging and dying in agony from a rough cross on this place called the Skull.

In the back of your mind lingers one question . . . *why?*

† EPILOGUE

W HY?"

That is *the* question.

Why receive the kiss from Judas without restraint? Why yield bare flesh to the merciless flagellum without resistance? Why accept the nails? Why would anyone submit to such pain by choice? Why would a man, innocent of all charges, willingly walk to an end reserved for the very worst of criminals?

It's a valid question—Why?

HIS PATHWAY PLANNED

It may surprise you, but the death of Jesus was planned long before it occurred. It was devised even before the Baby's cry in Bethlehem. And though man invented death by crucifixion, a much greater Being had a much deeper purpose in mind. As you read through the biblical account of the Passion story, you discover the ones who appear in charge: The Sanhedrin, Herod, the Roman guards, and even Pilate, are unknowingly following a borrowed script. Without realizing it, they assumed roles discussed long before in the early books of the

Bible. If you took the time to search the Scriptures, you would find numerous Old Testament prophecies, which are inescapable references to the death of Jesus.

One of the seven phrases Jesus uttered from the cross was, "My God, my God, why have You rejected Me?" Believe it or not, he was quoting from Psalm 22. Later in that Psalm we read more about His planned path:

> For dogs have surrounded me;
>> A band of evildoers has encompassed me;
> They pierced my hands and my feet.
>> I can count all my bones.
> They look, they stare at me;
>> They divide my garments among them,
> And for my clothing they cast lots.
>> Psalm 22:16–18, NASB

The Psalmist predicts that His hands and His feet would be pierced. None of His bones would be broken. His garments would be divided, and they would cast lots for His clothing. He would be the object of scorn and mockery. Remarkably, David penned all of those details over nine hundred years before they actually happened, right down to the final details.

After Jesus was crucified, Peter openly announced, "God said through the prophets that his Christ would suffer and die. And now God has made these things come true in this way" (Acts 3:18).

Unlike on the Passover night when Jesus's statements about His upcoming death confounded the impulsive disciple, Peter later remembered a prophet's statement written seven hundred years before the birth of Jesus:

> But it was the LORD who decided to crush him and make
> him suffer. . . . He will complete the things the LORD
> wants him to do.
>
> ISAIAH 53:10

Jesus was not actually murdered; He willingly gave up His life. One of the last phrases He said from the cross was "It is finished" (John 19:30). As Isaiah prophesied, Jesus completed the things His Father had planned for Him. Remember Gethsemane? "Take away this cup of suffering. But do what you want, not what I want." On the cross, Jesus "drank the cup"—He accomplished His God-given mission.

What was completed? What did He finish? And again, *why* did He go through all that?

OUR PATHWAY BLOCKED

Before we answer those questions, we need to address a serious issue: There's a roadblock on humanity's pathway to God. God desires that all people have a meaningful relationship with Him. But there is a problem wired into our genes. Put bluntly, we aren't good enough for God. We don't qualify.

> All have sinned and are not good enough for God's glory.
>
> ROMANS 3:23

Have you ever sinned? (Sounds like an archaic word doesn't it? It simply means any wrongdoing against God.) If you are like most folks, we tend to grade our sins. The small wrongs can be quickly counterbalanced by good deeds. A white lie can be covered by letting a neighbor borrow a ladder. The big ones, like murder, adultery, and embezzlement, take a bit more community service, but surely even they can be appeased.

Hell is reserved for a few really bad repeat offenders—the usual suspects: Hitler, Stalin, Pol Pot, and Osama Bin Laden. Most people picture God like the statue of the blind lady holding the scales of justice. He doesn't really see all that we do. Just as long as we make sure our good deeds balance out our evil deeds, we'll enter the heavenly country club.

There's only one problem: God never agreed to that plan.

The apostle Paul stated in Romans 6:23, "When people sin, they earn what sin pays—death." In God's plan, if we sin, we pay the price. And in God's plan that penalty is death.

God is all-powerful, all-knowing, and all-present. But there's one thing God cannot do: He cannot do anything against His eternal character. God is the only truly balanced being. He is perfectly gracious, and He is perfectly just. In His efforts to show grace, He cannot contradict His justice. Therefore if God decrees that the penalty for any infraction, or sin, against His holiness is death, that penalty must be satisfied before He can grant mercy. He cannot turn a blind eye to any sin, however large or small.

"So you're telling me that God rejects the guy who fudges a little on his tax return just as quickly as He does the guy who orders the death of millions?"

I'm not saying that . . . but God is.

THE PATHWAY OF HIS PASSION

God knew we could never remove the roadblock. With death as the penalty for sins, no amount of praying, going to church meetings, doing good deeds, or reading the Bible can sufficiently pay for our wrongs against God. The penalty needed to be paid for us if we hope to have a relationship with God. His character kept Him from ignoring our sin. So as a supreme act of His grace, God found a way to satisfy His justice—He took matters into His own hands, literally.

Epilogue

On a clear night in Bethlehem, God sent His Son to earth. The Baby cried and Jesus's mission began.

It finished with a death sentence—one reserved for us:

> But he took our suffering on him and felt our pain for us.
> We saw his suffering and thought God was punishing him.
> But he was wounded for the wrong we did; he was crushed
> for the evil we did. The punishment, which made us well,
> was given to him, and we are healed because of his wounds.
>
> ISAIAH 53:4–5

Isaiah states that God provided a substitute. On a hill outside Jerusalem, Jesus took our place and willingly paid the price for the sins of humanity, once and for all. That's *why* He died.

From the acts of injustice inflicted upon Jesus, God's justice was satisfied. As men poured out their wrath upon Jesus at His trials and his death, God's wrath against sin was completely released upon Him at the cross. All the wrath of God was poured out on Jesus when He bore our sins in His body on that cruel cross. By dying on the cross, Jesus paid the penalty we rightly deserve, forever removing the roadblock between us and God. As a result, the only thing that now separates humanity from a pathway to God is unbelief.

> God loved the world so much that he gave his one and only
> Son so that whoever believes in him may not be lost, but
> have eternal life. God did not send his Son into the world to
> judge the world guilty, but to save the world through him.
> People who believe in God's Son are not judged guilty.
> Those who do not believe have already been judged guilty,
> because they have not believed in God's one and only Son.
>
> JOHN 3:16–18

105

Fortunately for us, God's justice is balanced by His grace:

> But God shows his great love for us in this way: Christ
> died for us while we were still sinners.
>
> ROMANS 5:8

Remember Barabbas? Barabbas missed his cross because another Man literally took his place. In the same way, Jesus is our substitute too. He took our sins upon Himself and died the death that we deserve, just as He died the death that Barabbas deserved. He hung on the cross in our place just as He hung on that cross intended for Barabbas. Like Barabbas, we sit in the dungeon of our sin, awaiting our death sentence. Like Barabbas, we were condemned to die until Jesus took our place.

Jesus's pathway was planned with us in mind . . . planned by God so that you and I might have our sins forgiven. The death of Jesus opened the pathway to heaven—the pathway prepared and paved with His blood. His painful death at the cross revealed His eternal love for people like you . . . like me.

Now that we've answered the "why," what about *you?*

YOUR PATHWAY

You might have heard the story of His passion before, but this might be the first time you've heard the reason behind it.

The cross is the crux, the very basis, of Christianity. The cross distinguishes Christianity from every other religion:

- Other faiths demand that we pay the penalty for our own sins; Jesus paid that penalty for us.

Epilogue

- Other religions require that we ascend to God to be saved; in Jesus, God descended to save us.
- Other teachings expect us to earn our own way to God; Jesus cleared the path to God on our behalf.

Jesus put it so simply: "I am the way, and the truth, and the life. The only way to the Father is through me" (John 14:6). Have you ever wanted to get on that pathway to God? Ever wondered how to get started? Keep it simple. Just turn onto that path and walk. Earlier, I mentioned Romans 6:23; let me give you the rest of the verse:

> When people sin, they earn what sin pays—death. But God gives us a free gift—life forever in Christ Jesus our Lord.
>
> ROMANS 6:23

Think of it like this: In the courtroom of heaven, God has decided your sentence for your sin—death. You're guilty as charged. But Jesus offered His life in your place. His death satisfied God's demand. God now offers you a complete and permanent pardon. There's just one hitch: You must approach the bench and accept His gift of grace.

Perhaps you have never prayed to God about this before. Don't worry; He's waiting to hear from you. It's not the eloquence of your words, but rather the authenticity of your heart that matters. Here's a simple prayer you can pray:

Dear God,
I know that my sin has put a roadblock between You and me. Forgive me. Thank You for sending Jesus to die in my place. I trust in Jesus alone to forgive my sins. I now accept Your gift of eternal life. Thank You. In Jesus's name, Amen.

That prayer shows your desire to begin a relationship with God. If you prayed that prayer today, you're now on the pathway. The journey has just begun. I now recommend you do three things:

1. God gave you a Guidebook for your journey with Him. It's called the Bible. Start reading it today. You may even want to read more about Jesus by reading the first four books of the New Testament in your Bible—Matthew, Mark, Luke and John.

2. Find a church that teaches and believes the Bible is true and applicable to our daily lives. . . . start attending.

3. Call one of our pastoral counselors at Insight for Living. Call us today at (972) 473-5097 or visit us at www.insight.org, and we will be happy to celebrate your decision and send you some resources designed to help you begin your new journey with God.

Let me be the first to welcome you into the family of believers. What a wonderful decision you've made! Your new relationship with Jesus will bring about changes in your life from the inside out. As I wrote at the beginning, once you truly *Behold the Man* . . . you will never be the same again.

✝

*God loved the world so much that he gave
his one and only Son so that whoever
believes in him may not be lost,
but have eternal life.
God did not send his Son into the world
to judge the world guilty,
but to save the world through him.*

JOHN 3:16–17

ENDNOTES

CHAPTER THREE
THREE O'CLOCK IN THE MORNING

1. William Barclay, *The Gospel of Matthew, Vol. 2* (Philadelphia, Penn.: The Westminster Press, 1975), pp. 346–347.

CHAPTER FOUR
THE SIX TRIALS OF JESUS

1. Alexander Whyte, *Bible Characters* (Grand Rapids, Mich.: Zondervan Publishing House, 1952), p. 81.
2. Merrill C. Tenney, *The Gospel of John: The Expositor's Bible Commentary* (Grand Rapids, Mich.: Zondervan Publishing House, 1981), p. 176.

CHAPTER FIVE
THE MAN WHO MISSED HIS CROSS

1. James Stalker, *The Trial and Death of Jesus Christ* (Cincinnati, Oh.: Jennings and Graham, 1894), p. 87.

2. William Barclay, *The Gospel of Mark* (Philadelphia, Penn.: The Westminster Press; Edinburgh, Scotland: The Saint Andrew Press, 1975), p. 356. Used by permission of The Saint Andrew Press.

3. William Riley Wilson, *The Execution of Jesus* (New York, N.Y.: Charles Scribner & Sons, 1970), p. 141.

4. Ibid., pp. 141–142.

5. Barclay, *The Gospel of Mark*, p. 356.

Chapter Six
The Way of the Cross

1. Os Guinness, *The Call* (Nashville, Tenn.: Word Publishing, 1998), p. 79.

2. Jim Bishop, *The Day Christ Died* (New York, N.Y.: International Creative Management, 1957), p. 303. Used by permission.

Chapter Seven
The Darkest of All Days

1. Bishop, *The Day Christ Died*, pp. 320–321. Used by permission.

2. Merrill F. Unger, *Unger's Bible Dictionary* (Chicago, Ill.: Moody Press, 1957), p. 229.

3. Wilson, *The Execution of Jesus*, p. 152.

4. Bishop, *The Day Christ Died*, pp. 325–326. Used by permission.

5. Harvie Branscomb, *The Gospel of Mark* (1937), p. 292; as quoted in Wilson, The Execution of Jesus, p. 153.